D1524349

Praise For Aafia Unheard

"Aafia Unheard marks the first serious effort to tell the complicated and mysterious story of Aafia Siddiqui, and it is an excellent product. Dawood Ghazanavi, taking advantage of his expertise as a lawyer, uses legal documents and other key sources to piece together a fascinating narrative. What is particularly significant about Aafia Unheard is that it does not take a position on the case. Instead, it simply presents all the information and invites the reader to make his or her own conclusions. Ghazanavi's account does a masterful job of telling a story that is long overdue to be told, given its close connection to many hot-button issues ranging from the war in Afghanistan and the global war on terror to the volatile U.S.-Pakistan relationship."

- Micheal Kugelman Deputy Director, Woodrow Wilson Center

"Having investigated the troubling case of Dr. Aafia Siddiqui for more than 15 years now as a journalist, it is refreshing to see a new book on the subject. Aafia Unheard is probably the most comprehensive on the subject to date. It is also written in a style that lets the reader decide and draw their own conclusions. Ghazanavi has left no stone unturned in his search for the truth."

- Yvonne Ridley, British Journalist and Author

Also by Dawood Ghazanavi

Thinking Ahead : The Role of the Pakistani Diaspora in the 21ˢᵗ Century

AAFIA UNHEARD

"UNCOVERING THE PERSONAL AND
LEGAL MYSTERIES SURROUNDING FBI'S
MOST WANTED WOMAN!"

DAWOOD GHAZANAVI

First paperback edition 2019

Book design by Tayyeb Ali
Author Photograph by Ammara Nawaz Khan

Library of Congress Cataloging-in-Publishing Data has been applied for.

ISBN: 978-1-54397-380-8

Published by BookBaby
7905 N. Crescent Blvd.
Pennsauken, NJ 08110
https://www.bookbaby.com/

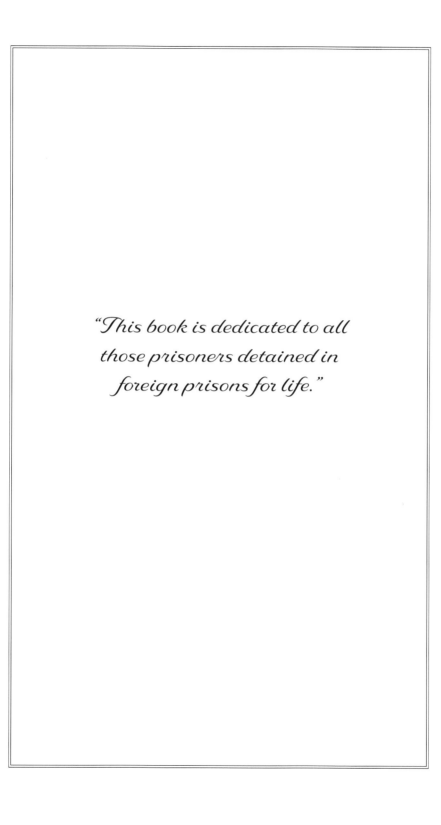

"This book is dedicated to all those prisoners detained in foreign prisons for life."

Foreword
Senator Dr. S.M. Zafar

The book *'Aafia Unheard'* is a heart rendering account of the suffering of an educated Pakistani woman and mother of three children into the dark corridors of prison facilities. The investigation has raised many questions regarding the trial and evidence in the case.

I, as the Chairman of the Standing Committee on Human Rights of the Senate, took notice of the press conference on 7th July, 2008 that Yvonne Ridley along with the current Prime Minister Imran Khan, Chairman PTI, held in Islamabad. After a number of meetings with authorities in the foreign office and the embassy in New York, we finally had access to prisoner No. 650 i.e. Dr. Aafia Siddiqui, whom I met along with a delegation of Senators in the Texas Federal Medical Centre (FMC) on 6 October, 2008.

Dr. Aafia was a weak shrunken lady who was answering some of our questions with complete composure, surrender, and calmness. Dr. Aafia informed us that she suffered torture both at the hands of Afghan guards and later 'foreigners' in the Bagram Cell. Her main complaint was the 'strip search' which she had to undergo each time that she had to come out or be taken back to her cell.

Now Dawood Ghazanavi has uncovered the personal and legal mysteries surrounding the most wanted woman (Prisoner No.650). Through the proceedings in the court and testimony of witnesses, Mr. Ghazanavi has taken readers through what Dr. Siddiqui suffered.

Table of Contents

Principal Characters

HONORABLE RICHARD M. BERMAN: United States District Judge of Southern District of New York

CHRISTOPHER L. LAVIGNE: United States Attorney of Southern District of New York

DAVID RASKIN: United States Attorney of Southern District of New York

DAVID RODY: United States Attorney of Southern District of New York

ELIZABETH M. FINK: Court Appointed Attorney for Dr. Aafia Siddiqui

DAWN M. CARDI: Court Appointed Attorney for Dr. Aafia Siddiqui

CHARLES D. SWIFT: Attorney for Dr. Aafia Siddiqui retained by the Government of Pakistan

LINDA MORENO: Attorney for Dr. Aafia Siddiqui retained by the Government of Pakistan

ELAINE WHITFIELD SHARP: Attorney for Dr. Aafia Siddiqui retained by the Government of Pakistan

TINA MONSHIPOUR FOSTER: Attorney for Dr. Aafia Siddiqui in 2255 Motion

ROBERT J. BOYLE: Attorney for Dr. Aafia Siddiqui in 2255 Motion

GORDAN HURLEY: Special Agent for Federal Bureau of Investigation FBI

DAWN CARD: Combat Medic for United States Army

ERIK NEGRON: Special Agent for Federal Bureau of Investigation FBI

CARLO J. ROSATI: Physical Scientist, Firearm and Toolmark examiner contracted to FBI laboratory

CHIEF WARRANT OFFICER: Command Special operations for the United States Army in Afghanistan

BASHIR: Working for Afghan Counterterrorism Department, Ghazni, Afghanistan

BRUCE KAMERMAN: Special Agent for Federal Bureau of Investigation FBI

ANGELA MICHELLE SERCER: Special Agent for Federal Bureau of Investigation FBI

JOHN JEFFERSON: Special Agent for Federal Bureau of Investigation FBI

AHMAD GUL: Working as Interpreter for United States Army

D.J. FIFE: Physical scientist, Forensic Examiner in the Latent Prints Operation Unit at FBI laboratory

AHMAD JAVID AMIN: Working as Interpreter for United States Army

KENNETH COOK: Sergeant First Class for United States Army

ROBERT LEE SNYDER: Captain in the United States Army

JOHN CALEB THREADCRAFT: Captain of the 101st Division in Ghazni for United States Army

BILL TOBIN: Expert in Material Science and Metallurgy retained by the Defense

FOWZIA SIDDIQUI: Dr. Aafia Siddiqui's biological sister

LESLIE POWERS: United States Government Forensic Psychologist who did Forensic Evaluation of Dr. Aafia Siddiqui

GREGORY B. SAATHOFF M.D: Forensic Psychologist retained by United States Government for Forensic Psychiatric Evaluation of Dr. Aafia Siddiqui

SALLY C. JOHNSON M.D: Forensic Psychologist retained by United States Government for Forensic Psychiatric Evaluation of Dr. Aafia Siddiqui

L. THOMAS KUCHARSKI: Forensic Psychologist retained by Defense for Forensic Psychiatric Evaluation of Dr. Aafia Siddiqui

Preface

Back in 2018, while fighting for the fundamental rights and repatriation of Pakistanis detained in Thailand and Sri Lanka (at the Islamabad High Court and Supreme Court of Pakistan), I came across the case history of FBI's most wanted fugitive lady Dr. Aafia Siddiqui. She is a woman who disappeared with her three children from Pakistan in 2003, and in 2008 was tried in the Southern District of New York on charges of attempted murder of American officials in Ghazni, Afghanistan. She was sentenced to 86 years and is currently incarcerated at the Federal Medical Center, Carswell, Fort Worth, Texas.

Due to my keen interest in understanding the relationship between our fundamental right to life, liberty, and life imprisonment, Dr. Aafia Siddiqui's case spoke to me.

I contacted Dr. Aafia Siddiqui's family and apprised the infringement of her fundamental rights while incarcerated at FMC, Carswell. Dr. Fowzia Siddiqui (Dr. Aafia's biological sister), under my legal assistance, filed a constitution petition under Article 184(3) of the constitution of Pakistan in the Supreme Court of Pakistan. It was prayed in the petition to direct the Government of Pakistan to offer assistance to its citizens especially Dr. Aafia Siddiqui, who was being held in deplorable conditions (while incarcerated in a foreign prison).

When it comes to Dr. Aafia Siddiqui, who is an M.I.T graduate and has a Ph.D. in neuroscience from Brandeis, her case is complicated. Ever since the U.S. Attorney General, John Ashcroft listed her name amongst the seven "most wanted" Al- Qaeda fugitives, she has been given many pseudonyms including "Lady Al-Qaeda" and "the Mata Hari of Al-Qaeda."

She has also been labeled an "operator and facilitator" for Al-Qaeda, willing to use her education against America. Many counterterrorism circles have linked her to the 9/11 ringleader Khalid Sheikh Mohammed and believe she was plotting mayhem on behalf of Osama Bin Laden. However, other credible sources refute all such accusations.

This range of 'for and against' opinions has made this woman the 21st century's most mysterious and controversial figures. I, like many other inquisitive people around the world, had many questions in mind. What was the case against her in the Southern District of New York? Was she kept in a US secret prison in Afghanistan during her disappearance from the year 2003-2008? Why did she testify in court despite strong reservations from her attorneys? Was she competent enough to stand trial in the U.S.A? Has her affiliation with Al-Qaeda or other terrorist organizations been established? Was she handed over to the U.S. without permission from Afghanistan President Hamid Karzai? Did Hussain Haqqani, the then Pakistani Ambassador in the U.S., meet the trial Judge in the Judge's Chamber during the trial proceedings? And so much more.

I wish to answer these questions while offering information through an unbiased lens. While there is a lot of Classified Information related to this case, I have tried to gather data from the US court files to present a clear picture. My research covers (08 CR 826) *United States of America v Aafia Siddiqui* case and (14 CV 3437) *Aafia Siddiqui v United States of America case* documents, the hearing transcripts, government and defense witness testimonies, and the court orders.

Dr. Aafia's testimony and narrative haven't been written or discussed in public before. Her narrative offers a unique perspective not cited in other books or documentaries. I wish to change that and give her voice a platform, too.

That is why I decided to give equal consideration to both the Government of the United States of America as well as Dr. Aafia's narrative. I hope, in doing so, you will be able to analyze facts and come to an informed conclusion regarding this case.

Dawood Ghazanavi

April 2019

Chapter 1

Dr. Aafia Siddiqui's Student Life In The USA From 1991-2002

W HEN TRYING TO UNDERSTAND SOMEONE, IT is crucial to start from the beginning. Due to the mystery and controversy surrounding Dr. Aafia Siddiqui's case, I think it is essential to go back to the basics related to her. Having such information might help you make an informed decision when it comes to how the legal system handled her and why there are still many questions people have about her.

In this chapter, I have explained Dr. Aafia's student years in the USA from Dr. Aafia's court testimony. Dr. Aafia said she was born in Pakistan and as a baby, she moved to Zambia, Africa to live with her father, who was working there as a physician. She shared she stayed in Zambia until the second grade. Her mother spent all of her life as a social worker and has worked with the APWA (All Pakistan Women Association).

Dr. Aafia told the court she was 17-years-old when she graduated from 12th grade in Karachi, Pakistan. After her graduation, she moved to the University of Houston (USA) for further education. She shared it was snowing when she arrived in Houston back in December 1991. Dr. Aafia was never sure what she wanted to study at the University of Houston, and therefore during her freshman year, she took as many courses as she could in the field of science, particularly chemistry and physics.[1]

Dr. Aafia always considered Chemistry as her weakest subject. She said the only C grades she had ever received in any subject was Chemistry which always brought her overall GPA down. She told the court she wanted to transfer from the University of Houston. That is why she took all her Chemistry courses at the University of Houston because she thought it couldn't have been easier anywhere else.

Dr. Aafia recalled her real interest was in Social Sciences, and not in traditional Science. But due to family pressure, especially from her mother, she had to do something in science. She said her mother always wanted her to be a doctor because other than her brother and herself everyone was a medical doctor in the family. And that is the reasons her mother wanted her to follow suit.

At the University of Houston, Dr. Aafia took part in nationwide essay competitions. She received an honorable nationwide award once in writing the best essay. The topic for the essay was "*How Intercultural Attitudes in America Helped Shaped a Multinational World.*" She stated there were many other awards she won during her time at the University of Houston.

She further stated after a year she left the University of Houston and transferred to the Massachusetts Institute of Technology (MIT), in Cambridge USA to finish her undergraduate studies. Dr. Aafia said that during her stay at MIT, she was very active with the public service center. She won two consecutive years of awards from the public service center. At the public service center, she worked and volunteered for children's education. She volunteered at the Martin Luther King Jr. School in Cambridge, MA, and taught children science. There she arranged a children's trip to MIT and many other places. She assisted the school in developing a curriculum on how to teach science because she thought they never had a set curriculum. She spent her spare time at the school, too.

Dr. Aafia said she also developed an adult education program, which was open to the public. The program became very popular, and many people started joining it after which she had to repeat the program numerous times. She won an award from MIT for her services to education. She said she also did an MIT sponsored research project on women's social issues in Pakistan.

Dr. Aafia graduated from MIT with a major in Biology. She picked up many courses concerning social sciences, as she was interested in anthropology gender issues, social issues, sociology, etc. She also took courses in Molecular biology, neuron and kinetic, as these were required to graduate with a Major in Biology. She said there were many courses which were required to graduate, but many were electives which she refused to take such as Microbiology, Human Physiology, and Immunology. She said she had A's in pretty much all of the Social Science courses.

At MIT she shared she worked with Nobel laureate Professor Noam Chomsky for one semester. She said he had wanted her to continue but she couldn't due to her academic load. Dr. Aafia shared she also worked with research topics related to human origin, religions, and science as well as studied comparative religion especially Asian Religions, Ethics, etc. After graduating from MIT, Dr. Aafia got admission at Brandeis University, Massachusetts in a Ph.D. program and also opted for a Master's degree along the way. She said both degrees were in Cognitive Neuroscience. Dr. Robert Secuda, a professor of Psychology, was Dr. Aafia's advisor at the University. She said she considered him a nice human being and still misses him.[2]

Dr. Aafia told the court her Ph.D. thesis was on "HOW CHILDREN LEARN BY IMITATION", in which she tested her hypothesis regarding alternate ways of learning. She said her hypothesis stated children would learn better by seeing how something is done versus being told how something is done. So, to prove her hypothesis, she used a computer, tablet, and stylus at the university lab. The children had to watch the movement of a ball & disk on a computer lab screen and then imitate the same actions. It was a form of imitation learning. Her conclusion was if you create an environment conducive to imitation learning, children who have difficulty in learning will be able to observe and learn quickly. She said she was able to prove her hypothesis was correct.

During her stay at Brandeis University, she gave birth to Ahmad and Meriam. She said after finishing her doctorate, she went to Pakistan in 2002 for a short visit and then came back to the USA. Dr. Aafia said when she came back to the US, she taught at a secondary school for a while. She stated her main concern was helping dyslexic children and the disabled who can't read and write very well, whom she thought were very intelligent and can learn. She wanted to design a system where these children could learn effectively. Dr. Aafia said she had her little playgroup and wanted to have a small school to teach kids there. Dr. Aafia told the court she again went back to Pakistan because her husband was there and they had their third child born named Soloman.[3]

Through Dr. Aafia's court testimony, you can tell she was a woman with a brilliant mind from a very young age. She belonged to a well-educated and respected family. She grew up in an environment which stressed education for both men and women. Furthermore, Dr. Aafia also had an empathic side to her and wanted to help make learning accessible for all.

How did such a woman end up where she currently is? What events did she go through before she was put on trial? Did she deserve the treatment she received? I have tried to answer similar questions and more in this book.

Chapter 2

Court's Attempt To Find Evidence On Dr. Aafia's Disappearance From 2003-2008

*T*HERE IS A PASSAGE OF TIME RELATED TO DR. Aafia's disappearance which many tried to make sense of when the case began in the trial court.

In this chapter, I have mentioned information from the court transcript which will help one analyze the court's attempt to find evidence on Dr. Aafia's disappearance from 2003-2008.

For Dr. Siddiqui's clinical treatment and assessment for competency to stand trial, Judge Berman asked both the government and defense attorney to apprise the court, if they are privy and have any information regarding Dr. Aafia's whereabouts from the period between 2003 and 2008. Judge Berman also asked for the information regarding the location of Dr. Aafia's three children.[4]

The Prosecution attorney Mr. LaVigne clarified to the court that in their direct case the government is not going to argue whether Dr. Aafia is a member of Al-Qaeda (or any terrorist organization) or that she has any such affiliations. Mr. LaVigne further stated they are not even going into any argument about whether Dr. Aafia was a member of Taliban or affiliated with Osama Bin Laden.[5]

Another prosecution attorney, Mr. Raskin, suggested that the court not hold a separate hearing to decide Dr. Aafia's whereabouts from 2003 to 2008. He stated for the record that they have read papers and heard various arguments and suggestions as well as have looked diligently at the question of what happened to Dr. Aafia between 2003 to 2008, and they have found zero evidence Dr. Aafia was abducted, kidnapped or tortured. He said the government doesn't know the basis for all such reports, as they have worked diligently with multiple agencies in the United States government and haven't found a shred of evidence those allegations are true.

He said they have evidence her oldest child, who was a boy, was captured along with her in Afghanistan. Mr. Raskin said the child was captured by local Afghan police, interviewed by them, and then subsequently interviewed by the FBI. He said the boy shared he was an orphan, disclaimed he had any familial relationship with Dr. Aafia, but confessed he was with her in Afghanistan. Mr. Raskin further said the FBI agent Almodovar was able to determine through Dr. Aafia's immigration file, from when she lived in the US, and then a subsequent DNA test to confirm the boy was Dr. Aafia's real son.

He said Dr. Aafia never claimed the boy as her son and the US government had to work extraordinarily hard with the Afghan authorities to find a proper home for the child. He said the boy was in an Afghan prison for a time and was never in US custody. Mr. Raskin said the boy was ultimately repatriated to Pakistan where he is with Dr. Aafia's family (currently). He said the government has reviewed all files and have found no information at all about the other two children as they were certainly not abducted by the US authorities. Mr. Raskin also added there is a suggestion Dr. Aafia went underground herself and was married to a man named

Ammar Al Baluchi, an Al Qaeda operative, who facilitated the 9/11 hijacking and terrorist attacks.

He said it is also reported she has connections with Khalid Sheikh Mohammed who was the mastermind of all the Al Qaeda operations. Mr. Raskin further said there was a trial in the same courtroom of a man named Uzair Paracha, who was convicted of participating in an Al Qaeda material support conspiracy and Dr. Aafia was a named co-conspirator in that case. He said that such allegations stem from her time here in the US, and she then due to the fact she went back to Pakistan. A series of arrests occurred in Pakistan in March, April 2003, and it was right after that Dr. Aafia disappeared.[6]

Mr. Raskin said there are allegations in Pakistan's press Dr. Aafia was abducted during that period. He shared there is a sort of equally or more plausible inference that Dr. Aafia went into hiding because everybody around her all of a sudden started to get arrested, and at least two or three of those people ended up in Guantanamo Bay.[7]

Mr. Raskin apprised the court there is no hard evidence available about where Dr. Aafia was during those years, but there are explanations from multiple angles. He also said an awful lot of evidence from the US Intelligence Agencies is classified, and if the court needs, there is a way to try get such classified information.[8]

Ms. Fink, a defense attorney, apprised the court that the child found with Dr. Aafia is Ahmad, and he is Dr. Aafia oldest son (and has just turned 12). She said he is under psychiatric care and heavily medicated as he was seriously disturbed. Ms. Fink said Ahmad lied to the US authorities about how he isn't related to Dr. Aafia and shared his parents were killed in an earthquake. She said Dr. Aafia's second child is Meriam who is an American National like Ahmad. She said it is entirely unknown where Meriam is as of yet.

She said there are many foreign human rights organizations and people who are looking for Meriam within Pakistan and overseas. Ms.

Fink also said it is her belief, based on information taken while talking to Pakistani press and various people, that in March 2003, while Dr. Aafia and her three children were on a taxi cab on their way to the Karachi airport to go to Islamabad to see Dr. Aafia's uncle, they were captured by the members of Pakistani intelligence agency ISI. Ms. Fink said the youngest child was six months old when Dr. Aafia was abducted in 2003. She said nothing is wholly known whether the child (a boy) is alive or was killed in captivity. She said this is all supposition by a number of people and none of it can be definitive. She said Dr. Aafia is not aware of these facts as she believes she only has two kids alive.[9]

Ms. Fink also apprised the court about the lawsuit in Islamabad High court which is looking into where Dr. Aafia and her children were from 2003-2008. She said a Pakistani Human Rights lawyer named Ghaffar had filed this suit and he has sent some data to this court too. Ms. Fink further noted that she is pretty clear Dr. Aafia was abducted. She can't figure out when Dr. Aafia was married to Ammar Al Baluchi because Dr. Aafia was in the US until 2002 working to get her Ph.D. at Brandeis. She said what she understands is that Dr. Aafia is an unindicted co-conspirator in the *Uzair Paracha case*, and she knows that Dr. Aafia's husband (Amjad Khan) had to do something with that case, and he was also under investigation by the FBI.

Ms. Fink said Dr. Aafia had only married Amjad Khan, who was an anesthesiologist, and it was an arranged marriage. Mr. Fink said Dr. Aafia only agreed to the arranged marriage on the condition she will be permitted to continue her education in the United States. She said the couple had three children from this marriage and they separated in 2002. Ms. Fink said she wouldn't go into details about why they broke up, but one of the main issues was about how their children should be educated. Ms. Fink said Amjad was a devout Muslim and wanted their kids to be taught under Muslim law whereas Dr. Aafia wanted her kids to be educated in the US.

Ms. Fink said Dr. Aafia's family was entirely unaware about Amjad's location. There had been news he went underground for a while. However, Ms. Fink said since Ahmad has been repatriated from Afghanistan to Pakistan, he is living with Dr. Aafia's sister Fowzia Siddiqui, who is taking care of Ahmed along with her three children. Dr. Aafia's mother Mrs. Siddiqui is living with them too. Ms. Fink said Dr. Aafia's family is an educated one. Her father was a doctor and was educated in England. Fowzia and their brother were also educated in the US.[10]

Chapter 3

Was Dr. Aafia In A Secret Prison From The Year 2003-2008?

*T*HE QUESTION ABOUT DR. AAFIA'S WHERE-abouts from 2003-2008 is an interesting one. Was she kept in secret prisons in Afghanistan during that time? Is there any undisputable proof supporting her assertion she was abducted?

These questions and more are what I hope to answer by presenting the required information accessible to me. In this chapter, I have mentioned in detail events which may lend credence to Dr. Aafia's assertion she was abducted and was kept in secret prisons in Afghanistan for many years. Dr. Aafia disappeared during the War on Terror era, and as per the prosecution, a lot of evidence by the US intelligence is still classified. Therefore, in this part of the book, I have relied on information made available to the public to precisely find out the truth about Dr. Aafia's assertion.

Following the September 11, 2001 attacks on the World Trade Center and the Pentagon, President George W Bush addressed the Joint Session of Congress and the American people on September 21, 2001.

The most prevalent extract of the speech was as such:

"On September the 11th, the enemies of freedom committed an act of war against our country. Americans have known wars, but for the past 136 years, they have been wars on foreign soils, except for the one Sunday in 1941. Americans have known the casualties, but not in the center of a great city on a peaceful morning. Americans have known surprise attacks but never before on thousands of civilians. All of this was brought upon us in a single day and night fell on a different world. A world where freedom itself was under attack. Americans have many questions tonight. Americans are asking, who attacked our country? The evidence we have gathered all points to a collection of loosely affiliated terrorist organization known as Al Qaeda. They are the same murderers indicted for bombing American embassies in Tanzania and Kenya, and responsible for bombing the USS Cole. The group and its leader, a person named Osama Bin Laden are linked to many other organizations in different countries. The leadership of Al Qaeda has its great influence in Afghanistan and supports the Taliban regime controlling most of that country. In Afghanistan, we see Al Qaeda's vision for the world. And tonight, the United States of America makes the following demands on the Taliban.

- Deliver to the United States authorities all the leaders of Al Qaeda who hide in your land.

- Release all foreign nationals, including American citizens, you have unjustly imprisoned.

- Protect foreign journalists, diplomats, and aid workers in your country.

- Close immediately and permanently every terrorist training camp in Afghanistan.

- And hand over every terrorist, and every person in their support structure to appropriate authorities.

- Give the United States full access to terrorist training camps, so we can make sure they are no longer operating".

President Bush said these demands were not open to negotiations or discussion, and the Taliban must act immediately and hand over the terrorists; otherwise, they will share the same fate as them. He also requested every country to join the US in its war against terrorism by asking the help of police force, intelligence services, and banking systems around the world.[11]

Taliban Ambassador to Pakistan Abdul Salam Zaeef had a news conference right after President Bush's speech. He said that without evidence, Afghanistan Taliban rulers would not hand over Osama Bin Laden. He said he was sorry people had died in the suicide attacks on the World Trade Center and the Pentagon. He further stated that if America has proof, then their government is ready for the trial of Osama Bin Laden in the light of the evidence.[12]

United States Deputy Secretary Armitage called in visiting Pakistani Intelligence (ISI) Chief General Mahmud and presented a "stark choice" in a 15-minutes long meeting. He said *Pakistan must either stand with the United States in its fight against terrorism or stand against us. There was no maneuvering room*". General Mahmud offered his and President Musharraf's condolences for this tragedy. He offered Pakistan's "unqualified support" that Islamabad would do whatever is required by the United States.[13]

Then Secretary Armitage told General Mahmud the United States is looking for full cooperation and partnership from Pakistan. Armitage presented General Mahmud with the following specific requests for immediate action and asked that he present them to President Musharraf for approval:

- Stop Al Qaeda operatives at Pakistan border, intercept arms shipments through Pakistan and end all logistical support for Bin Laden.

- Provide the U.S. with blanket overflight and landing rights to conduct all necessary military and intelligence operation.

- Provide as needed territorial access to the U.S and allied military intelligence, and other personnel to conduct all necessary operations against the perpetrators of terrorism or those that harbor them, including use of Pakistan's naval ports, airbases and strategic locations on borders.

- Provide the U.S. immediately with intelligence [EXCISED] information, to help prevent and respond to terrorist acts perpetrated against the U.S., its friends, and allies.

- Continue to publicly condemn the terrorist acts of September 11 and any other terrorist acts against the U.S. or its friends and allies [EXCISED].

- Cut off shipment of fuel to the Taliban and any other items and recruits, including volunteers en route to Afghanistan that can be used in a military offensive capacity or to abet the terrorist threat.

- Should the evidence strongly implicate Osama Bin Laden and the Al Qaeda network in Afghanistan and should Afghanistan and the Taliban continue to harbor him and this network, Pakistan will break diplomatic relations with the Taliban government, end support for the Taliban and assist us in the fore mentioned ways to destroy Osama Bin Laden.[14]

On September 19, 2001, President Musharraf addressed the nation with a statement about how thousands of lives have been lost in the wake of the terrorism in the United States for which he, the government of Pakistan and the whole nation are deeply grieved. He said right from the beginning till now, Osama Bin Laden and then Al-Qaeda movement are America's first target. He said their second target is the Taliban because they provide shelter to Osama Bin Laden and his Al-Qaeda network.

He said the third target is they intend to launch a prolonged war against international terrorism. He said in this entire campaign support is sorted from Pakistan, and the three important things in which Pakistan support is needed, firstly, exchange of intelligence and information, secondly, the use of Pakistan airspace and thirdly logistic support from Pakistan. He further said Pakistan is facing an extremely delicate situation and in his opinion, it is the most delicate phase since 1971. He said at this moment the Pakistan government decisions might have far-reaching and wide repercussions. He said in all of this Pakistan's critical concerns may be harmed by which he meant Pakistan's nuclear strength and the Kashmir cause.[15]

Pakistan did abandon its support for the Taliban government in Kabul and allowed US overflight rights. Pakistan also cooperated with the US intelligence services and deployed thousands of troops in the border area with Afghanistan in the hunt for Osama Bin Laden. President Musharraf said he balked at some of the US demands such as turning over border posts and bases to US forces.[16]

On October 02, 2001, President Bush again rejected the Taliban's appeal for discussion. He said there is no timeline for the Taliban just like there are no negotiations.[17] On October 07 2001, the US forces began strikes on terrorist camps of Al-Qaeda and the military installation of the Taliban regime in Afghanistan. About 40 nations were onboard with the United States nascent anti-terror coalition, all demonstrating varying degrees of cooperation. President Bush made a series of telephone calls to the world leaders including Pakistan President General Musharraf.[18]

The Bush administration on October 10, 2001, announced a new *"most wanted"* list of suspected terrorists. The *FBI Most Wanted Terrorists* list included the names of 22 suspected terrorists that included not only Osama Bin Laden and some of his top allies but also those thought to be responsible for a range of other deadly strikes. President Bush announced the list formally at FBI headquarters, accompanied by the FBI Director Robert Mueller, Attorney General John Ashcroft, and Secretary of State

Colin Powell. Attorney General Ashcroft said the new "most wanted list" will boost global publicity for the United States' manhunt and leave terrorists with "no place to hide."

The list identified only earlier-indicted defendants and no suspects in the attacks on the World Trade Centre and the Pentagon.[19]

Attorney General John Ashcroft then made a "9/11 Task Force" within the Justice Department to operate as the agency's central command structure for prosecuting terror cases involving the attacks on the World Trade Center and the Pentagon, and helping to prevent further acts of violence against the United States. The prosecution team was also tasked with gathering leads, information and evidence from around the world to centralize the effort to fend off future terror attacks.[20]

President Musharraf, in his memoir titled *In the Line of Fire*, shared how shortly after 9/11, many members of Al Qaeda fled Afghanistan and crossed the border into Pakistan and how Pakistan government had to play cat-and-mouse with them. He said the biggest name of them all was Osama Bin Laden who was still missing at the time he was writing his memoir, but they did catch many others. He said *"We had captured 689 and handed over 369 to the United States. We have earned bounties totaling millions of dollars."*[21]

On March 1, 2003, Khalid Sheikh Mohammed, the man believed to be the key planner of the terrorist attacks of September 11, 2001, was arrested by a CIA led operation in a house outside Islamabad, Pakistan. The arrest of Khalid Sheikh Mohammed was considered the single most important victory in the war against terror at the time. KSM was then taken to an unknown place the day he was arrested, and the officials in Pakistan were unaware of his whereabouts afterward.[22]

Then on March 5, 2003, US resident Majid Khan an Al Qaeda operative, and a direct subordinate to Khalid Sheikh Mohammed was also taken into custody from Pakistan by Pakistan's authorities. The same day the FBI authorized electronic surveillance of Majid Khan's residence in Maryland, United States.[23] According to a statement by Majid Khan's father the US and Pakistani agents interrogated his son for at least three weeks at a secret detention center in Karachi, Pakistan.[24]

On March 10, 2003, the FBI appeared at the door of Dr. Aafia's biological sister, Fowzia Siddiqui, in Baltimore, United States. Fowzia then phoned her biological brother Muhammad Siddiqui in Houston later that day and told him the FBI was looking for Dr. Aafia's whereabouts. Fowzia's brother called Annette Lamoreaux, an attorney for the American Civil Liberties Union then based in Texas, for advice and Lamoreaux agreed to represent him if the authorities contacted him again.[25]

On March 18, 2003, the Federal Bureau of Investigation (FBI) issued an ALERT NOTICE requesting information about Dr. Aafia Siddiqui[26]. The FBI, on their website, stated that Dr. Aafia Siddiqui's current whereabouts are unknown. The FBI believed she was in Pakistan. The notice also mentioned that the FBI has no information affiliating Dr. Aafia to any specific terrorist activities, but the FBI would like to locate and question her.[27]

It is pertinent to mention an incident here that in 2002, while Dr. Aafia and her ex-husband Amjad Khan (along with their kids) were on a weekend camping trip to Cape Cod and New Hampshire mountains in Boston, they went to a Boston camping store to buy hunting gear and supplies. Amjad purchased survival guides, a global positioning system, a night vision device for hunting and a bulletproof vest. Three or four weeks after the couple visited the camping store, the FBI appeared at their door. Dr. Aafia was at home. She heard the FBI at the door but refused to open it for them. She phoned Amjad at work, and he barely hung up when two FBI agents appeared at his workplace. The FBI agents did minor questioning with him. Then Amjad called a Boston attorney, James Merberg who made an appointment with the FBI agents for Dr. Aafia and her husband. The FBI agents asked some questions to Dr. Aafia and Amjad. They wanted to know about the camping equipment and the night vision device Amjad had bought. The FBI asked if Amjad had ever met Osama Bin Laden and he replied no. The agent asked Dr. Aafia about giving charity to certain Muslim organizations in the USA, to which Dr. Aafia replied that it was her duty to offer charity. The agents made an appointment with them to meet again in a few weeks. During this time, Dr. Aafia's father fell ill again. He had suffered two heart attacks in recent years. This time Dr. Aafia needed to be with him in Pakistan. She was also six months pregnant, and if she waited longer to travel, she wouldn't be allowed on the plane. James Merberg advised Dr. Aafia and Amjad to postpone their departure long enough to attend the second meeting. But at the end of June 2002 both went to Pakistan.[28]

At trial, the prosecution attorney during cross-examining Dr. Aafia did ask a series of questions to her regarding the meeting with members of the FBI in 2002. Question number one was, whether Dr. Aafia was questioned by the FBI shortly before she left for Pakistan in 2002. Aafia answered in a yes. She said the FBI came to question her ex-husband, and in that connection, they did talk to her also, but they were not there to question her.

Question number two was, whether she left the United States about a week after that conversation with the FBI. Again, Dr. Aafia replied with a yes. She said they did leave the United States within that time, but it was instead a coincidence because she was leaving the United States anyway. Question number three was whether she left the United States because she knew she was wanted for questioning by the FBI. Dr. Aafia said this wasn't the case at all.[29]

On or around March 28, 2003, a Pakistani citizen named Uzair Paracha, was arrested in New York City and was charged in the Southern District Court of New York, with other unknown people, with conspiracy, confederate, an agreement with each other to provide "material support or resources" to a foreign terrorist organization.[30]

In March of 2003, Dr. Aafia divorced her husband Amjad Khan and was staying at her biological mother's (Ismat Siddiqui) house along with her three children (Ahmed, Meriam and six months old Soloman). On March 26, 2003, against her mother wishes, Dr. Aafia announced she was leaving the house. Dr. Aafia's mother cried and screamed at her to stay, but she went anyways, in a minicab. Ismat Siddiqui later stated that "Aafia took all three children with her that day." Ismat said Dr. Aafia told her she and her three children were going to Islamabad to stay with her uncle S.H. Faruqi. Ismat said Dr. Aafia planned to stop on the way to visit friends in Rawalpindi whom Ismat didn't know. She said Dr. Aafia did call her from what she believed was the Karachi train station, but Dr. Aafia never arrived at her Uncle Faruqi house.[31]

Dr. Aafia's Uncle S.H. Faruqi, in his letter published in Dawn Newspaper, explained that Dr. Aafia on learning of the campaign of the FBI regarding her went underground in Karachi, and remained so till her kidnapping apparently by the FBI hired intelligence personnel in Pakistan, at the end of March 2003.

He added that between March 25, 2003 and March 31, 2003, Dr. Aafia rang up her mother from some location in Karachi informing her about her intentions to go to Rawalpindi. He further added that during that time Urdu Daily published the news of her arrest by the police while she was on her way to the Karachi airport. He said at the time of her kidnapping her three children accompanied her, aged between seven years, three and a six months old.[32]

On March 29, 2003, Pakistani and United States news media began airing a confusing series of on-again, off-again reports that Dr. Aafia had been arrested[33]. On March 31, 2003, another source, a news reporter Azfarul Ashfaque from "The News International," reported a story that a woman who was on FBI's list of having suspected links to Al-Qaeda had been taken into custody by the sleuths of sensitive agencies in Karachi, Pakistan. He said according to sources it was suspected the woman was

Dr. Aafia Siddiqui and she was picked up from a house in Gulshan-e-Iqbal area on Friday, March 28, 2003. He mentioned in the report that Dr. Aafia was spotted by the law enforcement agency personnel at the Quaid-e-Azam International Airport, Karachi while returning from upcountry, and chased by them and finally arrested from the house of her relatives. He said after her arrest she was then taken to an undisclosed location where initially she was interrogated by local investigators and then on March 29, 2003, the FBI agents were allowed to question Dr. Aafia. He further shared Pakistan government officials in Karachi and Islamabad were reluctant to confirm the news of the detention of Dr. Aafia.[34] On March 31, 2003 another news agency named Kuwait News Agency (KUNA) reported a story that a Pakistani woman, who was on the US Federal Bureau of Investigation (FBI) most wanted list, suspected of having links with "Al Qaeda" terror network had been captured in the Eastern Pakistani port city of Karachi. The report said a security official told KUNA by telephone from Karachi that Dr. Aafia Siddiqui, a Ph.D. doctor was picked up from a house in downtown Karachi by law enforcement agency personnel. The report further said she was traced by the law enforcement agency person-nel at the Karachi International Airport, after returning from abroad, and was taken to an undisclosed location where initially she was interrogated by local investigators and then by FBI agents.[35]

Ismat Siddiqui told BBC news reporters that two days after Dr. Aafia and her three children went missing, "a man wearing a motor-bike helmet" arrived at her home in Karachi. She said he didn't take off the helmet, but he told her if she ever wanted to see her daughter and grandchildren again, she should keep quiet."[36]

It should be noted, elected Prime Minister of Pakistan (in the 2018 general elections), Imran Khan has followed Dr. Aafia's case since her Uncle S.A Faruqi in 2003 called him for help. Imran Khan shared his con-versation with Ismat Siddiqui on Pakistan TV talk show named "Off the Record" which aired on ARY Digital on February 3, 2010. He said during Dr. Aafia disappearance in March 2003, he called Ismat Siddiqui and offered to do a press conference with the family and ask the Pakistan government about Dr. Aafia's disappearance, but he said Dr. Aafia's mother was terrified and said security agencies are threatening them on the phone that if the family makes any noise they will kill her daughter.[37]

Back on April 21, 2003, NBC Nightly News channel got exclusive details from NBC Senior Investigative Correspondent Lisa Mayers about Dr. Aafia's whereabouts. Lisa Mayers said a senior US official shared with her that Dr. Aafia is a 31-year-old mother of three, educated at MIT and Brandeis, is in custody and being questioned by Pakistani authorities about possible ties to Al-Qaeda. She said the FBI posted Dr. Aafia's name and picture on its terrorism website a month ago. Furthermore she said senior U.S. officials believe that Dr. Aafia has ties to radical individuals in Pakistan. While not an actual member, she may be working as a fixer for Al Qaeda, someone who has been used to move money and provide other logistical support. She said he further told that Dr. Aafia had not been charged with any crime, and her family lawyer has denied any link to terrorism, but if she is helping Al Qaeda, then she would be the first ever woman tied to that group[38]. Yet the following day of this news, the US officials backed off, saying they were "doubtful" that Dr. Aafia was in custody. They offered no explanation for the bizarre and continuing confusion, and Dr. Aafia's picture remained on the FBI website. Then on April 24, 2003, the FBI issued another warning that Al Qaeda might start using women in attacks.[39]

In April 2013, Ammar al Baluchi, nephew of the alleged 9/11 mastermind Khalid Sheikh Mohammed, was captured in Pakistan by Pakistani authorities and was handed over to the US.

A US Senate Intelligence Committee report stated Ammar Al Baluchi was taken to a notorious CIA black site known as the Salt Pit, near Kabul.[40] During the period of his arrest, the US government also claimed Ammar Al Baluchi and Dr. Aafia married shortly before his capture.[41]

In June 2003, "Washington Times" newspaper interviewed FBI Baltimore based Special Agent Barry Maddox. During the interview, Barry Maddox showed unawareness of the *Newsweek magazine* cover story, which stated Dr. Aafia was apprehended in Pakistan.[42]

In Pakistan, the country's Ministry of Interior, through its spokesperson, confirmed Dr. Aafia was handed over to the United States because she had kept her US nationality. The spokesperson further said Pakistan interrogated her, but her links with Al Qaeda could not be established.[43]

In June 2003, during Camp David Press talks between President Bush and President Musharraf, President Bush remarked that since September 11, 2001 attacks, Pakistan has apprehended more than 500 Al Qaeda and Taliban terrorists, through effective border security measures and the law enforcement cooperation throughout the country and then thanked Pakistan and especially the leadership of President Musharraf.[44]

In 2004, U.S. Attorney General John Ashcroft and FBI Director Robert Mueller made another announcement that intelligence from multiple sources has indicated Al Qaeda intends to attack the United States in the coming months. They said they are seeking help from the American people to be on the lookout for seven individuals including Dr. Aafia Siddiqui that were associated with Al Qaeda. They requested the people that if anyone had any information about any one of the seven, then they must report it to law enforcement.[45]

Uzair Paracha, who was arrested in New York City in 2003, got a conviction on March 23, 2005, by the Southern District Court of New York on charges including conspiracy to provide material support to the Al Qaeda foreign terrorist organization and identification document fraud committed to facilitating an act of international terrorism. The conspiracy within the case was explained in the press release by the United States Attorney Southern District of New York. The detail of the press release is as follow:

"The evidence at the trial proved that Uzair Paracha, 26, agreed with his father, Saifullah Paracha, and two Al Qaeda members, Majid Khan and Ammar Al-Baluchi, to provide support to Al Qaeda by among other things, like trying to help Majid Khan obtain a travel document that would have allowed Majid Khan to re-enter the United States to commit a terrorist act. Statements from Majid Khan while detained at Guantanamo Bay admitted at trial revealed that, once inside the United States, Majid Khan intended to carry out an attack on gasoline stations in Maryland. Uzair Paracha also posed as Majid Khan during telephone calls with the Immigration and Naturalization Service (now Immigration and Customs Enforcement), and called Majid Khan's bank, and attempted to gather information about Khan's immigration paperwork via the Internet. Uzair Paracha also agreed to use Majid Khan's credit card to make it appear that Khan was in the United States, when in fact Khan was in Pakistan. Uzair Paracha and his father had discussed with Majid Khan and Al-Baluchi the possibility of the Paracha's receiving up to $200,000 from Al Qaeda in connection with the assistance Paracha was providing to Khan, which the Paracha hoped to invest in their businesses."

The Press release further stated that in 2003 the detectives of the New York Joint Terrorism Task Force while interrogating Uzair Paracha, also found in Uzair Paracha's possession a number of identification documents belonging to Majid Khan, including Majid Khan's driver's license, Majid Khan's Social Security card, Majid Khan's bank card and a handwritten list of instructions from Majid Khan directing Uzair Paracha on how to pose as Majid Khan when making inquiries with the INS. The Task Force also found in Uzair Paracha's possession a key to a post office box opened in Majid Khan's name by Aafia Siddiqui in Maryland, which Uzair Paracha was to check to see if Majid Khan's immigration documents had been delivered.[46]

Dr. Aafia was cleared as an unindicted co-conspirator in the Uzair Paracha case, but in 2008 US prosecutors did file a formal letter in the Federal court holding out the possibility they might charge Dr. Aafia in connection with opening the post office box for Majid Khan, but they never did so.[47]

Dr. Aafia's Uncle S.H. Faruqi's wrote another letter to *Dawn* newspaper, in which he explained that since Dr. Aafia's return to Pakistan in 2002, she failed to get a suitable job, and she again visited the US on a valid US visa in February 2003, to search for a job and to submit an application to the US immigration authorities. He said she moved freely in the US and came back to Karachi by the end of February 2003 after renting a post office box in her name in Maryland for her mail.[48]

In 2005, *Washington Post* staff writer Dana Priest broke a story about how the CIA has been hiding and interrogating some of its important Al Qaeda captives at secret facilities overseas. The existence and location of the facilities were referred to as "black sites," and these sites were part of a covert prison system set up by the CIA nearly four years ago. The story indicated that these sites existed in eight countries, including Thailand, Afghanistan and several democracies in Eastern Europe, as well as a small center at the Guantanamo Bay prison in Cuba. It also indicated that this hidden global internment was dependent on the cooperation of foreign intelligence services, and on keeping even basic information about the system secret from the public, foreign officials and nearly all members of the U.S. Congress charged with overseeing the CIA's covert actions.[49]

Human Rights organizations discovered the *"enhanced interrogation techniques"* used by CIA interrogators at these black sites. The CIA itself drew up a list of interrogation techniques that included sleep deprivation, slapping, subjection to cold and simulated drowning, known as "waterboarding."[50]

Two psychologists were paid more than $80 million by the CIA to develop these "enhanced interrogation techniques."[51] The Senate Intelligence Committee report on CIA torture concluded that such enhanced interrogation techniques were brutal and far worse than what the CIA presented to the policymakers and others.[52] The Committee's investigation found that CIA routinely misled the White House and the Congress about the information it obtained, and failed to provide the basic outsight of the secret prisons it established around the world.[53]

Dr. Aafia during a direct examination at the trial did mention her time at a secret prison. Dr. Aafia's exact statement from the court transcript follows:

The COURT: *Relax. What do you want to say?*

Dr. Aafia: *I never – I was under the impression that these – because before I was brought – before they rearrested me, Americans, it was standard practice of the people who were keeping me, they were also Americans, they looked like American, they spoke like them, I call them fake Americans, they were acting against the USA in the guise of Americans. I stop at that.*

MS Sharp: *Your Honor*

Dr Aafia: *But what they were doing for so many years was giving me information, telling me this is just a game, you are not the only one, doctor, whoever –*

MS Sharp: *Objection*

Dr Aafia: *We know how to do experiments on you, and they would tell me information and then make me repeat it in front of a different group of people who would interrogate me, question me repeatedly hundreds of times. So if I messed up, it was torture. I thought it was the same game.*

The COURT: *The objection is sustained. We will strike this.*

MS Sharp: *No your honor, I move for mistrial on the ground that the government has elicited the last five years and denied us classified information.*

The COURT: *The application is denied. Please Continue.*

MS Sharp: *Thank you, Your Honor.*

The COURT: *So we are talking about –*

Dr Aafia: *Angela does not know that. I thought this was a game again. I did not know who I was speaking to. If I knew this is the real FBI, I am in the hands of real official American agencies, I would be happy to tell them, look, help me get children. You know? And since then I have been trying to reach you; I want to give you a statement explaining this.*

The COURT: *Next Question.*

Dr Aafia: *So, whatever I told you, you have to understand, it's what those people under threat of killing and raping my daughter wanted me to say. And it was always a game. It was never real. But this time I guess it was. I don't understand it, but that's how war works now[54].*

The parliamentarians at the Council of Europe set up an investigation following reports in the US media the CIA had been operating secret detention centers for terror suspects in Europe. The final investigation report in 2006 named more than 20 countries (including Poland and Romania) that had cooperated with a program of secret CIA flights moving suspects to and from the so-called "black sites."

In January 2006, the European Parliament set up a separate inquiry led by Claudio Fava, an Italian MPE. His report concluded the CIA operated nearly 1,245 flights through European airspace between 2001 and 2005.[55]

Open Society Foundation created the Open Society Justice Initiative which formulated a report under the name "*Globalizing Torture of CIA Secret Detention and Extraordinary rendition.*" The report showed 54 countries who participated in the CIA secret detention and extraordinary rendition operations. These countries included Afghanistan, Albania,

Algeria, Australia, Austria, Azerbaijan, Belgium, Bosnia-Herzegovina, Canada, Croatia, Cyprus, the Czech Republic, Denmark, Djibouti, Egypt, Ethiopia, Finland, Gambia, Georgia, Germany, Greece, Hong Kong, Iceland, Indonesia, Iran, Ireland, Italy, Jordan, Kenya, Libya, Lithuania, Macedonia, Malawi, Malaysia, Mauritania, Morocco, Pakistan, Poland, Portugal, Romania, Saudi Arabia, Somalia, South Africa, Spain, Sri Lanka, Sweden, Syria, Thailand, Turkey, United Arab Emirates, United Kingdom, Uzbekistan, Yemen, and Zimbabwe.[56]

In response to these accusations by Human Rights organizations, Ms. Condoleezza Rice, then US Secretary of State, said "Rendition is a vital tool in combating transnational terrorism...renditions take terrorists out of action, and save lives."[57]

Finally, in 2006, President Bush acknowledged the existence of secret CIA prisons and said 14 key terrorist suspects had been moved out of CIA custody and would face trial. These suspects include the alleged mastermind of the 9/11 attacks Khalid Sheikh Mohammed who had been moved out of CIA custody and would face trial.[58]

An extract of President Bush's September 06, 2006 speech on "military commission to try suspected terrorists" is:

"In this new war, the most important source of information on where the terrorists are hiding and what they are planning is the terrorists, themselves. Captured terrorists have unique knowledge about how terrorist networks operate. They have knowledge of where their operatives are deployed and knowledge about what plots are underway. This intelligence -- this is intelligence that cannot be found any other place. And our security depends on getting this kind of information. To win the war on terror, we must be able to detain, question, and, when appropriate, prosecute terrorists captured here in America, and on the battlefields around the world. After the 9/11 attacks, our coalition launched operations across the world to remove terrorist safe havens and capture or kill terrorist operatives and leaders. Working with our allies, we've captured and detained thousands of terrorists and enemy fighters in Afghanistan, in Iraq, and other fronts of this war on terror."[59]

In 2007, in a briefing before the US Congress House Committee on Foreign Affairs, Michael F. Scheuer, the former chief of the Bin Laden Unit for the CIA addressed the issue of rendition and the CIA's Rendition Program. At one point he stated, "After 9/11 and under President Bush, rendered Al Qaeda operatives have been most often kept in US custody. No rendered Al Qaeda leader has ever been kidnapped by the United States. They have always first been either arrested or seized by a local security or intelligence service."[60]

International Justice Network, a US-based non-profit organization providing legal assistance to survivors of human rights abuses and their families, released a transcript which was a secretly recorded conversation between Syed Bilal, an American citizen residing in Texas, with Imran Shauqat the Superintendent of Police for Sindh, Pakistan. Shaukat told Bilal he personally participated in Dr. Aafia's March 2003 abduction. He said she was stick thin and also crazy with American demeanor when she was apprehended. He said she was wearing gloves and a veil. When she was caught she was traveling to Islamabad. He said we handed her over to ISI and took her children with us. He additionally told Bilal that Dr. Aafia was eventually handed over to American Agencies.[61]

In Harper's Magazine, an article *"The Intelligence Factory"* was written by Petra Bartosiewicz. In this article Petra narrated one incident involving her being meeting retired Pakistani ISI officer in the following words:

"One afternoon in Islamabad she met a recently retired senior Pakistani Intelligence officer who had promised if she agreed not to name him, will answer all her questions. She said they spoke at his home, a gated mansion in one of the city's wealthiest precincts. She said he had silver hair and a silver mustache, and he wore a gold pinky ring fitted with a large green stone. She said when she called to arrange the interview, he initially said he did not know why Aafia has disappeared. But he then contacted a friend in Pakistan intelligence agencies who had been "pretty senior in the hierarchy" when Siddiqui disappeared in 2003. Then over the customary drinks and cookies, the retired intelligence officer recounted his conversation with his ISI friend, and said that Aafia had in fact been picked up by the Pakistani intelligence and delivered to "the friends" which was short-hand, he said for the CIA."[62]

Moazzam Begg, a British citizen who was abducted from Pakistan in 2002 and handed over to the USA, and was incarcerated in Bagram detention center and Guantanamo for three years, was released by the US without charges in 2005.[63] In 2006, Moazzam Begg became the first prisoner to give a book-length voice to the experience of being on the other side of America's war on terror. Begg's memoir detailed the three years he spent as a U.S. held detainee in Afghanistan and Guantanamo Bay.[64]

In his memoir, Moazzam Begg narrated an incident of a woman while he was in Bagram detention center, Afghanistan. He said:

"I began to hear the chilling screams of a woman next door. My mind battled with asking questions which I was too afraid to learn the answer to. 'What if it was ...... my wife?'

For two days and nights, I heard the sound of the screaming. I felt my mind collapsing, and contradictory thoughts ran through it.

Once I thought, when the screams started up, 'I am just going to slip my wrists out of the shackles, hit the guard, grab the weapon off him, and go next door to stop what is happening.' But my other thought was 'just give them whatever they want.'

At the end of it all, I asked them, 'Why have you got a woman next door?' They told me there was no woman next door. But I was unconvinced. Those screams echoed through my worst nightmares for a long time. I later learned in Guantanamo, from other prisoners, that they had heard the screams too and believed it was my wife. They have been praying for her deliverance. The memory of those screams was even worse than the physical humiliation."[65]

Dr. Aafia, at three different occasions in the trial, during direct and cross-examination, clearly mentioned her detention at a secret prison.

DIRECT EXAMINATION

MS Sharp: Dr. Siddiqui you talked about being in a secret prison. Were you tortured in that secret prison?

Dr Aafia: Yes

MS Sharp: When you were at Bagram Craig Joint Theater Hospital were you afraid that that was going to happen to you again?

Dr Aafia: Yes

MS Sharp: When it was suggested to you that torture was or we will hand you over to someone else – someone else, is that what you were afraid of?

Dr Aafia: This was actually something very --- I don't know how to say -- different from my past experiences with the secret prison. But you know I was still definitely --- definitely afraid of that. Yes. In some ways it was different. So I was very confused as a result of --- I was confused as a result of this, but yes, definitely, that was the fear I had[66].

DIRECT EXAMINATION

MS Sharp: I notice just a moment – I notice that you are adjusting your veil.

Dr Aafia: Because I have no pin, nothing to fix it with.

MS Sharp: What is it called?

Dr Aafia: The material is pretty

MS Sharp: What is this veil? What is it called?

Dr Aafia: I don't know. It is a scarf. I don't know if it has a name.

MS Sharp: Is that part of your religion?

Dr Aafia: Yes

MS Sharp: How is it part of your religion? I want the ladies and gentlemen of the jury to understand why you are wearing a veil

Dr Aafia: Okay. It is that, too. There is a personal thing attached, too. If you have been in a, I don't know, secret prison, abused, you get --- you become a bit more modest. That's all[67]

CROSS-EXAMINATION

MS DABBS: Now, this document discusses the construction of the dirty bomb, right?

Dr Aafia: I don't think so

MS DABBS: Well ---

Dr Aafia: I don't know. See, I don't write this stuff. You have to understand if you are in prison and --- I mean, that is what I ask is that people need to understand that if they are in the secret prison, their kids are tortured in front of them, they don't know how to do things they are asked to do. The worse they do is copy something from a magazine. Is that a crime?

THE COURT: This is not responsive. We will strike this[68].

Yvonne Ridley, an experienced journalist, had covered conflicts around the globe. She had worked for the Sunday Times, the Observer and the Independent and had covered stories in Cyprus, Damascus, Lockerbie, Afghanistan and Northern Ireland.[69]

She was the Chief Reporter on an undercover assignment in Afghanistan immediately after 9/11 and became the subject of international headlines when she was held by the Taliban.[70]

When Yvonne Ridley read the facts about a woman screaming in secret prison in Bagram, from Moazzam Begg's memoir *"Enemy Combatant,"* she began reinvestigating his claims, and started finding credible evidence about whether CIA was holding any woman prisoner in its secret prisons. She was even given a copy of the interview recorded by an Arab man, who escaped Bagram in July 2005, and was clearly talking about seeing a woman in US custody. The statement given in the interview was recorded as such:

"She stayed in solitary confinement for two years in Bagram prison among more than five hundred men. She stayed until she lost her mind, and became insane, hitting the door, and screaming day and night."[71]

Then in 2007, Human Rights Watch, Amnesty International and several other human rights groups included Dr. Aafia Siddiqui on a 2007 list of people suspected to have been in CIA custody.[72]

Answering the question about whether CIA was holding any women in secret prisons, Yvonne Ridley was reaching out and investigating at greater length for some time, and then later discovered from another one-time prisoner at Bagram that he also had seen a woman at secret prison in Bagram, and he said the Americans had given her the number 650. Ridley doubted at first Dr. Aafia could be prisoner 650, but whoever prisoner 650 was, Ridley wanted to find out more.[73]

Ridley began calling the lady as the "gray lady of Bagram." Ridley then personally spoke with Lt. Co. Mark Wright at the US Pentagon who denied all knowledge of Prisoner 650. Ridley told Lt. Col., Mark Wright, that she didn't believe he was lying to her, in fact Ridley suggested to him the people he was speaking to in Afghanistan (CIA) might be lying to him. She asked him to call her back once the facts were clear.[74] Later Ridley told Lt. Co. Mark Wright stopped answering her call, and the movie made by the Bagram escapees which had appeared on the internet for two years was pulled down.[75]

CAGE formerly Cageprisoners, is a UK based independent organization striving for a world free of injustice and oppression. Yvonne Ridley is one of the patrons for Cageprisoners.

Cageprisoners has led the campaign for Dr. Aafia since her disappearance in 2003. In July 2008, Ridley traveled to Pakistan with Cageprisoners' director Saghir Hussain, when called for help for a Pakistani woman she believed was being held in isolation by the Americans in their Bagram secret prison for over four years. She urged every Pakistani to ring America, ask them who Prisoner 650 is. She wanted them to ask: What is her crime? Who else is being held illegally? How many secret detention centers are there?[76]

On July 6 July 2008, Ridley held a joint press conference with the Chairman Pakistan Tehreek e Insaf (PTI) political party Imran Khan (current Prime Minister of Pakistan) in Islamabad, Pakistan. More than 100 journalists attended the press conference, and Imran Khan pledged his full support to Ridley's mission.

On July 11, 2008, Lt. Col Rumi Nielson Green, Director of Public Affairs wing of the U.S. forces at the Bagram base in Afghanistan denied that any woman prisoner was detained at their bases. He was responding to the press conference held recently by Imran Khan and Yvonne Ridley. Lt. Col Rumi claimed the US valued human rights and their detention operations comply with American law. He said the International Committee of the Red Cross (ICRC) made regular visits to the facilities and detainees. When he was asked if any woman had been held from 2002 onwards or if there were women in other detention facilities in Afghanistan, he said, "he will have to refer the complaint to the U.S. Department of Defense for any historical questions or perhaps to the ICRC." Col Rumi never responded to a request to check prisoner records and identify "Prisoner 650."[77]

Then on July 17, 2008, Dr. Aafia Siddiqui, who had gone missing from the city of Karachi five years earlier, suddenly emerged with her son outside the Governor of Ghazni, Afghanistan compound. Later on July 18, 2008, Dr. Aafia was shot in an Afghan police headquarter Ghazni while allegedly trying to attack US soldiers and officials.[78]

Islamabad was abuzz with rumors about the presence of Dr. Aafia in one of the US's most notorious secret prison in Bagram. Many assumed Dr. Aafia must be Ridley's Prisoner 650. Pakistan Home Secretary Syed Kamal Shah and other senior home ministry officials had denied the presence of such a lady in Bagram. Media reports continued to suggest she was extradited to the Afghan jail from Karachi with her children.[79]

On August 01, 2008 Lord Nazir Ahmed, member of British House of Lords, staged a protest outside Pakistan embassy, London and questioned Pakistani authorities with these words, "We want to know what happened to Dr. Aafia from March 31, 2003, until July 17, 2008."[80]

On August 08, 2008 the Asian Human Rights Commission released a photo of crumbled Aafia, lying down with her eyes closed and what appeared to be swollen lips and broken nose.[81] The Asian Human Rights Commission claimed that "a closer look at the picture shows evidence of the years of physical abuse, with dark circles under her eyes, and her nose apparently broken at some stage and has been badly set".[82]

Dr. Aafia Siddiqui's family lawyer in the U.S., Elaine Whitfield Sharp, told CNN the scenario was utterly implausible, saying, "This is a very intelligent woman. What is she doing outside of the Governor's residence? This woman is a Ph.D. Is a woman like this really that stupid? There is an incongruity, and I have trouble accepting the Government's claim."[83]

Yvonne Ridley in her documentary *"In Search of Prisoner 650"* narrated that suddenly after Dr. Aafia's arrest the Pentagon capitulated and admitted that Prisoner 650 did exist and was released in January 2005 to her country of origin. Ridley said it was a major breakthrough, but then the US said it was not Dr. Aafia Siddiqui. Ridley further said the officials tried to assure her that her research for the Gray Lady of Bagram was concluded, but she was not convinced and thought this was just the beginning.

She returned to Pakistan again in October 2008 and asked for the help of people of Pakistan to find the Gray Lady of Bagram. She attended a huge Muslim rally organized by Jamaat-e-Islami and appealed to Pakistanis to find "Prisoner 650." Ridley interviewed Dr. Ghairat Baheer, who served as the Afghanistan ambassador to Pakistan. He was also abducted from Pakistan in the middle of the night in 2002 and was held by the US for six years without any charges. He was regarded as a high profile detainee because of his close links to Afghanistan Prime Minister Golbadin Hikmatyar. Dr. Baheer was held in several dark sites, but he was eventually taken to a secret prison in Bagram. During the interview he narrated his time at Bagram in the following words:

"When I was in secret prison in Bagram, we used to have one lady prisoner, whose presence in the jail was heartbreaking for all of us, when she was put backward and forward by American soldiers, it was against our culture and our religion. I couldn't ask her full identity but she was in solitary confinement, she was my neighbor for couple of weeks. She used to be taken to showers, to doctor to interrogation in public in front of all the detainees, but finally, it was understood almost by every detainee that she was losing her mind, she was finally mentally disturbed, and she was not acting properly. I didn't see any more women in Bagram than this woman."[84]

In February 2009, a British resident Binyam Mohamed was released from US custody after the UK government's intervention. In 2002, he was handed over to US custody by Pakistan authorities. He was put on a CIA plane and secretly transferred to Morocco. In 2004 he was transferred to the 'secret prison' in Afghanistan, where he said he was tortured for a prolonged period, including being hung upside down, being chained up, and being exposed to non-stop deafeningly loud music. In 2004, he was taken to Guantanamo Bay where he was held in solitary confinement.[85]

Cageprisoners published an interview with Binyam Mohamed in 2009. Moazzam Begg conducted the interview. In a portion of the interview, Moazzam Begg focused on a few questions regarding the people Binyam Mohamed witnessed being held in custody by the US secret prison in Bagram, and specific questions about "Prisoner 650." Binyam Mohamed stated he saw prisoner 650 several times and heard the guards speaking of her multiple times on different days. The prisoners were told not to talk to her because she was a spy from Pakistan and the US had brought her to Bagram. They knew she was a Pakistani but was educated in the USA. When Moazzam Begg showed a picture of Dr. Aafia to Binyam Mohamed, he affirmed she was the woman wearing the shirt with 650 on it, and she was in isolation. He said she seemed to be very disturbed and literally out of her mind. Binyam didn't feel she was sane at that point.[86]

On PRESSTV, Yvonne Ridley did an interview with Binyam Mohamed. He said again that Prisoner 650 was Dr. Aafia Siddiqui. He said in Bagram he didn't come across any female prisoner except Dr. Aafia.[87]

In 2010, right after Dr. Aafia's conviction in Southern District New York, her daughter Meriam was mysteriously found outside of her grandmother Ismat Siddiqui's house in Karachi. It was reported some unknown people left her there with a collar bearing the address of the house 'in case she wandered off.' It was also confirmed the girl was Dr. Aafia's missing daughter, as her DNA test came positive. The details of her missing period, spread over seven long years, and the identity of the unknown people, who left her near her mother's residence, remains a mystery.[88]

The rendition of hundreds of suspected Al-Qaeda members from Pakistan held in secret prisons around the globe does offer some proof to Dr. Aafia's assertion to the extent that people were picked up from Pakistan and were kept in secret prisons. It can be seen that during 2003-2008 both the U.S. and Pakistan officials have made contradictory statements regarding Dr. Aafia's disappearance and during one instance Pakistan's Ministry of Interior spokesperson confirmed Dr. Aafia was handed over to the U.S. government because she had U.S. nationality, but the U.S. government categorically denied detaining Dr. Aafia in their custody at any time. In fact, the U.S. government had always denied detaining any female prisoners at their secret prions. However, at one point, admitted that a woman, Prisoner 650, was detained in Bagram, Afghanistan until 2005 yet claimed she was not Dr. Aafia.

Dr. Aafia's reappearance in Ghazni, Afghanistan soon after Yvonne Ridley and Imran Khan's press conference was surprising. Even in the court when it was asked whether the US government detained Dr. Aafia from 2003-2008, the prosecution informed the court an awful lot of evidence with the US intelligence agencies was classified. It can also be seen the trial court was once interested to know Dr. Aafia's whereabouts from 2003-2008, but during direct and cross-examinations whenever Dr. Aafia referred to herself being detained in a secret prison, her testimony was disjointed by the court. It is also interesting to add that Khalid Sheikh Mohammed, Majid Khan, Saifullah Paracha, Ammar Al Baluchi who were also named in a conspiracy in the Uzair Paracha case were taken into custody from Pakistan during the same month when Dr. Aafia disappeared.

It can be seen how Dr. Aafia's assertion, taking into account the accessible information, she was abducted from Karachi, Pakistan does hold weight for some. However, this can only be confirmed once the US agencies declassify relevant information from 2003-2008.

Chapter 4

The United States Of America Case Versus Dr. Aafia's Testimony

*D*URING THE TRIAL AT THE SOUTHERN District Court of New York (SDNY), Dr. Aafia was represented by the court-appointed attorney Ms. Dawn Cardi and three private attorneys (Elaine Whitfield Sharp, Charles Swift, and Linda Moreno) retained by the Government of Pakistan on Dr. Aafia's behalf. According to US law, Dr. Aafia had no obligation to testify, but she decided to testify as a defense witness despite the strong reservations by her attorneys. Being a defendant in a criminal case, Dr. Aafia even had no obligation to prove her innocence because it was a burden on the government to prove her guilt beyond a reasonable doubt. The court advised Dr. Aafia that during a criminal case if the defendant decides that it is not in their best interest to testify and doesn't testify, then the jury can't hold that against the defendant in any way.[89] Dr. Aafia understood the court guidelines, but she still decided to stand in the witness box.

In this chapter, Dr. Aafia's witness testimony has been compared with the United States of America Government case against her. The chain

AAFIA UNHEARD ★ 45

of events explained by the United States of America government in the case has also been examined in the light of Dr. Aafia's testimony.

UNITED STATES OF AMERICA CRIMINAL COMPLAINT AGAINST AAFIA SIDDIQUI

On July 31, 2008, Mehtab Syed, Special Agent of the Federal Bureau of Investigation (FBI) filed a criminal complaint before the Honorable Theodore H. Katz, United States Magistrate Judge Southern District of New York. In the criminal complaint, the FBI charged Dr. Aafia of unlawfully, willfully and knowingly using a deadly and dangerous weapon and did forcibly assault, resist, oppose, impede, intimidate and interfere with the officers of the FBI and armed forces, who were on their official duties. The FBI also charged Dr. Aafia on attempt to kill the officer and employees of the FBI and the United States armed services, who were on their official duties.

Special Agent Mehtab Syed explained in the criminal complaint the basis of her knowledge and for the foregoing charges in part was she was the special Agent for FBI Joint Terrorism Task Force (JTTF) and she has been involved personally in the investigation of this matter. She said she was familiar with the facts and the circumstances explained in this criminal complaint from her personal participation in the investigation, including her examination of reports and records, and her conversations with other law enforcement officers and other individuals.

Special Agent Mehtab Syed then explained in the complaint that based on her review of FBI and other law enforcement reports, as well as witness statements, and based on her conversations with the law enforcement officers; she has learned the following:

Dr. Aafia Siddiqui was a Pakistani national who had previously lived in the United States. On or around the evening of July 17, 2008, officers of the Ghazni Province Afghanistan National Police (ANP) discovered a Pakistani woman, later identified as Siddiqui, along with a teenage boy, outside the Ghazni governor's compound. ANP officers questioned Siddiqui in the local dialects of Dari and Pashtu. Siddiqui didn't respond and appeared to speak only Urdu, indicating that she was a foreigner. Regarding Siddiqui as suspicious, ANP officer searched her handbag and found numerous documents describing the creation of explosives, chemical weapons and other weapons involving biological material and radiological agents. Siddiqui's papers included the description of various landmarks in the United States particularly in New York City, documents detailing United States military assets, excerpts from the Anarchist's Arsenal, and one gigabyte (1GB) digital media storage device (thumb drive). Siddiqui was also in possession of numerous chemical substances in gel and liquid form that were sealed in bottles and glass jars.

On or about July 18, 2008, a party of United States personnel, including two FBI special agents, a United States Warrant Officer (the "Warrant Officer"), a United States Army Captain (the "Captain") and United States Military interpreters, arrived at the Afghan facility where Dr. Aafia Siddiqui was being held. The personnel entered a second-floor meeting room. A yellow curtain was stretched across the length of that room, concealing a portion of the room from sight. None of the United States personnel were aware that Siddiqui was being held, unsecured, behind the curtain. The warrant officer took a seat with a solid wall behind him and the curtain to his right. The warrant officer placed his United States Army M-4 rifle on the floor to his right next to the curtain, near his right foot. The weapon was loaded with the safety on. Shortly after the meeting began, the captain heard a woman's voice yelling from the vicinity of the curtain. The captain turned to the noise and saw Siddiqui in the portion of the room behind the curtain, which was now slightly pulled back. Siddiqui was holding the Warrant Officer's rifle and pointing it directly at the captain. The captain heard Siddiqui say in English, "May the blood of (unintelligible) be directly on your (unintelligible, possibly head or hands)." The captain saw one of the interpreter ("Interpreter 1") who was seated closest to Siddiqui, lunge at Siddiqui and push the rifle away as Siddiqui pulled the trigger. The warrant officer saw and heard Siddiqui fire two shots as Interpreter 1 tried to wrestle the gun from her. No one was hit. The warrant officer heard Siddiqui exclaim "Allah Akbar." Another interpreter ("Interpreter 2") heard Siddiqui yell in English, "Get the fuck out of here" as she fired the rifle. The Warrant Officer returned fire with a 9 mm service pistol and fired approximately two rounds at Siddiqui's torso, hitting her at least once. Despite being shot Siddiqui struggled with the officers when they tried to subdue her, she struck and kicked them while shouting in English that she wanted to kill Americans. Interpreter 2 saw Siddiqui lose consciousness. The agents and officers then rendered medical aid to Siddiqui.[90]

UNITED STATES OF AMERICA CASE VERSION AT TRIAL

On or around September 2, 2008, an indictment was filed against Aafia charging her with seven counts, including 1- Attempted murder of United States nationals in violation of 18 U.S.C. section 2332(b)(1) and 3228; 2- Attempted murder of United States officers and employees in violation of 18 U.S.C. section 114(3) and 3238; 3- Armed assault against United States officers and employees in violation of 18 U.S.C. section 924(c)(1)(A)(iii), 924(c)(1)(B)(ii) and 3238; 5- Assault against United States officers and employees (Interpreter 1) in violation of 18 U.S.C. section 111(a)(1) and 3238; 6- Assault against United States officers and employees (FBI special Agent 1) in violation of 18 U.S.C. section 111((a)(1) and 3238; and 7- Assault against United States officers and employees (U.S. Army officer 2) in violation of 18 U.S.C. Section 111(a)(1) and 3238. Each offense is alleged to have occurred on or about July 18, 2008, at an Afghan National Police headquarters in Ghazni, Afghanistan.

During the Trial, the United States personnel, including FBI special agents John Jefferson, Erik Negron, Angela Sercer, and Bruce Kamerman, a United States Chief Warrant Officer (the "Warrant Officer"), the United States Army Captain Robert Lee Snyder and Captain John

Caleb Threadcraft, a combat medic Dawn Card, the United States Military Interpreters Ahmad Gul and Ahmad Jawid Amin, and finally Afghan counterterrorism department employee Bashir, gave their testimony in court, to prove United States of America case against Aafia. FBI Agents Negron and Jefferson, Captain Snyder, Interpreters Gul and Amin, Chief Warrant Officer, and Military Medic Dawn Card gave testimony as the eyewitnesses of July 18, 2008 shooting event at an Afghan National Police compound in Ghazni, Afghanistan. Captain Threadcraft and Bashir gave testimony as witnesses of the first account of items found in Aafia Siddiqui's possession when she was arrested on July 17, 2008, by the Afghan law enforcement agencies outside Ghazni Governor Compound. Angela Sercer gave testimony of an interview she conducted with Dr. Aafia, and Bruce Kamerman gave testimony of incriminating statements made by Dr. Aafia during her stay at the Craig Joint Theater Hospital, Bagram, Afghanistan, from July 19, 2008, to August 3, 2008. The US government's case against Aafia majorly revolves around the testimony of these witnesses.

On July 17, 2008, a woman (later identified as Aafia Siddiqui) was caught by Afghan National Police (ANP) officers near Ghazni Governor Compound and was taken to the Ghazni National Police headquarters. The woman was arrested along with a little boy. She was wearing a burka when the ANP officers arrested her. The ANP handed her over to Afghan counterterrorism department, as it was the duty of the other department to keep such persons in custody and to interrogate them. The counterterrorism department took the woman to its office for interrogation. Bashir was involved in the interrogation as he could speak Urdu and hence was used as an interpreter. When Bashir spoke with her in Urdu, she responded in Urdu. The interrogation team asked her the reason for her presence in Ghazni. She did not give any information. They asked her questions about the documentation and items they found in a bag in her possession. As Bashir went through the documents, he found two copies of the documents, one in English and the other in Urdu. The documents were all about how to make bombs. Bashir thought that anybody who gets his hands on these documents could easily make a bomb. The other items he found from her bag were bottles, pants and some cosmetics, but there were some other substances, too. During further interrogation the woman mentioned her name first as Dr. Ali, and that she went to school until 8th grade. When interrogators asked her to write something in Dari, she could only write a few lines. Bashir asked her who she was taking these documents to. She said that she had given a copy of these documents to some people in Parwar which is in the Kabul Province, and she wanted to give some of them to some other people in Ghazni province while the master copy was supposed to go to Hara Province. Bashir asked her why she brought this documentation to Afghanistan, to which she said that we are not against the Afghanistan police or Afghanistan military, but she was against the foreigners. At one point during interrogation Bashir was sitting with the head of counterterrorism in his office when he heard her whispering to the little boy, that he must do or say the same thing as she was doing or saying. During the interrogation, she also tried to escape and threatened Bashir that she has a bottle in her hand, and if he doesn't release her, she will blow herself up. Bashir grabbed her from behind and got her down to the ground, during the struggle she bit Bashir's wrist, and the little boy also came and bit Bashir's hand. Basher called the head of counterterrorism and another person to prevent her from running away. They managed to stop her from running away and made her sit on the bed although she continued to kick and punch. At this point, Bashir hit her two or three times. Bashir told her that since she is a female, they look at her as a sister. The interrogating team didn't have handcuffs in their office, and they used a scarf to tie her hands behind her back. Bashir took the boy in the other office to further interrogate him[91].

At 9 pm, on July 17, 2008, Ghazni Governor Usman telephoned Captain Threadcraft. In Afghanistan, Captain Threadcraft was working as a liaison officer with the Afghan National Security forces (ANSF) at the Provincial Coordination Center (PCC) Ghazni. Governor Usman informed Threadcraft that a female bomb-maker had been captured, and he was coming to PCC to meet him. When Governor Usman came to PCC, he took Threadcraft to his bedroom and asked everyone to leave the room. The governor closed the door and pulled out a purse (evidence). He flipped the purse upside down and emptied the contents on the floor in the middle of the room. He picked up one item at a time and handed it over to Threadcraft and asked him if he can see what it is. Threadcraft read over each item and put it in another stack. When both finished going through the papers, governor Usman started to pick up other contents of the purse and started showing them to Threadcraft. The documents were written in a different language as Threadcraft could have read Dari, and that (the said documents) were not written in Dari. Governor Usman told him that it was Urdu. And they had a couple of guys around them who could speak Urdu. There were some documents written in English, and it was written: "dirty bomb" and something worded like Ebola. Threadcraft remembered seeing something in the items which looked to him like a fuse. He also saw pictures within the documents that looked like a mosque. Governor Usman told him that it was actually a mosque in Ghazni. Threadcraft also saw a plastic jar with a lid on top, and it had a white substance inside and even found some kind of makeup and some facial cream or something resembling a makeup pad. He also found some woman clothing. Governor Usman also gave him a thumb drive and told Threadcraft they had found all this from a woman's purse who they have arrested today during the hours of limited visibility outside his compound. Threadcraft went out of the bedroom, and took the thumb drive to the Tactical Operations Center (TOC) and handed it over to Sergeant Beard to put it on his computer and see what was in the drive. When Threadcraft saw the things in the drive, it made him feel like there was a threat.

Threadcraft went back to his bedroom and asked Governor Usman to put all of the things back in the purse and not to touch them any further as there can be poison and also because he does not want any more fingerprints on it. Threadcraft said goodbye to Governor Usman and went back to Tactical Operations Center where he called Battalion Commander

Lieutenant Colonel Anthony DeMartino and told him everything. Lieutenant Colonel DeMartino gave Threadcraft recommendations that the US must take this woman into custody to ensure she will be protected, as they have female guards and medics which would be more appropriate. Lieutenant Colonel DeMartino further told him to do what he thought was best. Threadcraft then got into an ANP vehicle, loaded up US soldiers into the armored truck and drove over to the ANP headquarters. Threadcraft took the purse with him, too. When Threadcraft walked into the compound of the ANP headquarters, there was a large crowd around a room. He assumed that was the room where the female detainee was being held. He went through the door and walked inside. Inside the room, he saw the Police Chief was sitting on one of the two bunk beds in the room. Threadcraft then noticed a female handcuffed to the bed along with a little boy. The Police Chief asked everyone to go out except Threadcraft and another person who could speak Urdu. Threadcraft sat on the bed to which the prisoner was handcuffed, and the person who could speak Urdu began talking to her. Then Threadcraft stood up from the bed, went to the Police Chief and asked him to release the female to US custody. The Police chief refused. Threadcraft asked the Police Chief that if he would release her if the Governor told him to do so. The Police Chief said yes. Threadcraft then went to the Ghazni governor's compound, took the Governor into one of the guestrooms and explained to him the situation and asked for the woman's custody. The Governor agreed and said he would go with him to the Police Chief right then. He got up, and both went to the ANP headquarters. During this whole ordeal, the purse was with Threadcraft. When they reached ANP headquarter, both of them went to the woman's room. This time the Governor spoke with the woman briefly, and then both came out of the room. After the meeting, the Governor, Threadcraft and some other people present there, sat down on chairs outside along with the Police Chief and began talking. The Governor narrated the story of how she had been detained. He started telling the story in an Afghani culture in a way to honor the guy who brought her into custody. Threadcraft appreciated him saying he did a good job. When the Governor finished the story, they again asked the Police Chief his permission to take the woman. The Governor said he is giving his permission. To this, the Police Chief said he could not release her unless the Minister of Interior (MOI) specifically tells him to release her into US custody. Threadcraft then spoke with Minister of Interior who refused to release her at such a late hour of the night. Governor Usman then told Threadcraft that tomorrow after the press conference in ANP headquarters, unless President Hamid Karzai refuses to release her, he will hand over the woman to US custody. The governor then asked Threadcraft to bring the purse and its contents tomorrow at the press conference. In response Threadcraft said he would instead bring copies of it as he believed it would be best not to have 10, 20,30 more people handling the contents and putting their fingerprints on the content. Governor Usman agreed. Threadcraft stayed at the police headquarters until about 2 am in the morning. Threadcraft then reached Fort Operating Base (FOB), Ghazni. He turned over the purse and its contents to the S2 shop, which is the Intel and Security shop in FOB. The S2 shop's job was to document things, take pictures, and then handle contents. At the S2 shop Threadcraft met Lieutenant Scheppler, Captain Snyder and some of the young men who were running around taking care of things. Threadcraft gave the thumb drive to Lieutenant Shappler and took the purse into the conference room which had a long table. He started to lay out all of the purse's contents there. Everybody present put gloves on before handling the content. Threadcraft had his interpreter who could speak Pushtu, Dari, Urdu, and English start translating all the Urdu documents into English.[92]

Captain Snyder then notified the Special Forces Team and the Chief Warrant Officer to come to the conference room. The Chief Warrant Officer came early morning of July 18, 2008.[93] When he came to the conference room and saw the items spread on the table, he became as confused as others were initially. He said he had never seen anything like that in Afghanistan, and he thought it seemed there might be an American in custody of the Afghanistan security. Chief Warrant Officer then talked with Captain Snyder a little bit and said they needed to inform the Federal Bureau of Investigation (FBI).[94] He believed the FBI had capabilities on the investigative side and their crime lab.[95] Chief Warrant Officer was then put in contact with the FBI.[96] Captain John Kendall at the FBI received Chief Warrant Officer's call. John Kendall then contacted FBI Agent Negron and told him that Afghan National Police had a woman in their custody, how she might be of interest to the FBI, how she had been discovered with some formulas on her, and that they would like the FBI to go out there and interview her. Agent Negron then notified Captain Kendall and Major Russell he wished to go out there with Agent Jefferson. Major Russell recommended taking Staff Sergeant William with them, too. Before getting on the aircraft to Ghazni, both agents gathered their sensitive site exploitation equipment to take with them. The different equipment included fingerprint equipment, DNA collection equipment, and evidence bags.[97]

Both FBI agents arrived at FOB, Ghazni by Black Hawk helicopter at 11:00 am on July 18, 2008. They were picked up by the Chief Warrant Officer, who took them to the FOB headquarters.[98] Upon their arrival a meeting took place inside the Special Forces Headquarters where they planned the tactical mission to travel to Ghazni's Governor.[99]

On the morning of July 18, 2008, Captain Snyder, Colonel DeMartino and a few of the senior staff officers of Captain Snyder battalion were scheduled to go to the Ghazni Governor compound for an unrelated weekly meeting with the Governor to talk about security and their operations and how they could better support them. When Captain Snyder brought the situation to Colonel's attention, the plan was made to include the Warrant officer with a member of his team and the FBI team to ask the Governor for permission to question the detainee.[100] The FBI agents wanted to bring the woman back and interview her at Bagram.

The reason why they were trying to bring her back was in case the Afghanistan government moved her to another location which might not be accessible to them. At about noon, Captain Snyder and his interpreter

Amin, Colonel DeMartino along with 20 personnel from his battalion, the two FBI agents, Chief Warrant officer with his interpreter Gul and ten members from Special Forces, headed towards Governor Usman's compound in Ghazni. They traveled in a convoy consisting of armored vehicles which included three MRAPs and also two Hummer vehicles. Chief Warrant officer, the two FBI agents, and interpreter Gul sat in one vehicle. Governor Usman greeted them all and started his conversation initially about how he was having problems with the Taliban. The conversation then moved to the woman detained at ANP. They asked to meet the woman, and the FBI requested to take her back to Bagram. The Governor denied their request and told them he could not allow this as President Hamid Karzai was en route to Ghazni to attend to this matter and has not allowed them to give her to US custody. The Governor said the FBI could interview her, take her fingerprints and DNA swab, but she would not be released into their custody. After the meeting they all left the Governor's compound for FOB, leaving Colonel DeMartino to negotiate with the Governor on other matters.[101] They all had another meeting at FOB, and Chief Warrant officer asked the FBI what exactly they wanted to do with a woman.[102]

Agent Negron made a phone call to his senior officer and advised him on the entire situation. The senior officer told him they need to go back and at least interview the woman, obtain her fingerprints and also conduct a DNA swab. Agent Negron contacted the Chief Warrant Officer and told him the FBI agents want to go back to ANP headquarters and interview that woman.[103] The chief warrant officer agreed to take the FBI agents to the ANP headquarters to meet the woman. The Chief Warrant Officer informed Colonel DeMartino he was taking the FBI agents to meet her. Once again at approximately 1:00 pm, Captain Snyder along with his interpreter Amin, Sergeant first class Cook, Pat MacDonald his law enforcement professional, Chief Warrant Officer along with his interpreter Gul, members from Special Forces, FBI agents Negron, Jefferson, specialist Army Medic Dawn Card and staff Sergeant Williams traveled to the Afghan National Police headquarters in a configuration of convoy consisting of three MRAPs and two Humvees.[104] Captain Snyder had an Army combat uniform, an M4 rifle, a M9 pistol, helmet, ammunition, water, night vision goggles, and bulletproof plates on the front and the back.[105] Agent Negron and Jefferson were wearing military fatigues and were carrying an AR 15 rifle, Glock Pistol and a 9-millimeter. The Special Forces also had Army combat uniforms.[106] Chief Warrant Officer was wearing an Army combat uniform, body armor, boots, helmet, an M4-A1 rifle with 5.56 – 5.56 x 45 Millimeter rounds and a M9 pistol.[107] Medic Dawn Card had a helmet, flat vest, an M4 rifle, an aid bag drop bag which consisted of medical supplies such as IVs and Kerlix two by fours.[108] Interpreters Amin and Gul had on Army combat uniforms and an AK-47.[109] Staff Sergeant Williams was wearing body armor, helmet, peltors, gloves, an M4 rifle and a M9 pistol[110].

When the convoy reached the ANP headquarters Ghazni, everyone in the convoy parked the vehicles inside the ANP compound.[111] The ANP headquarters is located in the middle of the Ghazni city and is surrounded by a concrete wall. The concrete wall was approximately 7 feet tall. Within the concrete wall, there were several two-story buildings with a garden area situated between the buildings.[112] Sergeant Cook and Pat MacDonald along with Special Forces Unit secured the ANP door outside. It was like posting security to the door just to secure the building. They put sergeant Scherbinki on the machine gun mounted on top of the Humvee and oriented him to the area they wanted to secure in the ANP headquarter. There were a minimum of 150 to over 200 Afghan personnel roaming around the ANP courtyard with various sized weapons like AK-47s.[113]

When Captain Snyder, interpreters Amin and Gul, Sergeant Cook, Williams, FBI agents Negron, Jefferson, Pat MacDonald, and Dawn Card went inside the ANP headquarter, they spoke to some of the representatives of the headquarter and tried to find out where the woman was being kept. The ANP representatives told them no senior officials such as Chief of Police were available at the headquarters and that is the reason they could not allow them to see the woman.[114]

At this point, Chief Warrant Officer along with FBI agents went into the second-in-command officer's room. Chief Warrant Officer informed the officer they had a meeting with the Governor of Ghazni and they have requested him that they want to interview the woman in custody to confirm whether she was an American citizen or not. He also notified the officer that Governor Usman had permitted them to interview the woman to confirm or deny whether or not she was an American citizen. The officer made a couple of phone calls and got back to Chief Warrant Officer saying he would let them do what they wanted, but first, they must go upstairs (of the building) to the counterterrorism office and speak with the gentlemen from the Ministry of Interior. Chief Warrant Officer was also told the woman was in a jail cell. Specifically, he was told she had been chained (all four limbs), because they couldn't control her.[115]

Captain Snyder, Pat Macdonald, Sergeant Cook, Sergeant Scherbinski and interpreter Gul, all decided to contact the representatives of National Director of Security (NDS) in ANP headquarters. NDS is the Intelligence apparatus of Afghanistan government. They contacted one of the representatives who attempted to contact Colonel Jassim, the Headquarter Chief. After some time, NDS representative returned and started discussing with Sergeant Cook and Pat MacDonald. After that Pat MacDonald told Captain Snyder they would be taken to the place where the woman was detained. Captain Snyder immediately followed Sergeant Cook and Pat MacDonald. They all went to the back entrance of the ANP headquarters building with NDS representative who motioned them to enter a room and then had them follow him into the building. Inside the building, they followed a NDS representative to the second floor where they were led to a room which had a sheet covering the entryway. At this point, only Captain Snyder, interpreter Amin, and Sergeant Williams entered the room. Sergeant Cook and Pat MacDonald went downstairs to the entryway of the building for security.[116]

Chief Warrant Officer along with his interpreter Gul, and FBI agents followed the second-in-command officer to speak with the two gentlemen from the Ministry of Interior located in the counterterrorism office of the ANP compound. They all walked toward the counterterrorism office together and proceeded up the stairs and entered the room. When they entered, they found Captain Snyder along with his interpreter and some gentlemen sitting in the center of the room dressed very nicely. They could tell these gentlemen were not from Ghazni by their dress, so they assumed they were the Ministry of Interior officers.[117] Army Medic Card first stood in the doorway because she felt uncomfortable going in the room due to a lot of people there. But then Pat MacDonald told her it looked rude to stand in the doorway and she needed to go in and sit, which she did.[118]

It was a poorly lit large rectangular room with dark carpeting.[119] To the right of the room, there was a filing cabinet, some chairs and coffee tables with a window behind them. To the left was a desk at an angle with the chair.[120] Directly across from the door was another window wall with chairs in front of it. To the left of the window was a photo of President Hamid Karzai on the wall.[121] Behind the desk in the center of the room was a yellow curtain that went from one wall to the end of the other wall. The curtain separated the room into two halves.[122] Behind the curtain there was a bed next to the small window.

The room was crowded in fact, when Chief Warrant Officer and FBI agents entered the room, the Chief Warrant Officer had to look for an available seat. He got a seat right under President Hamid Karzai's picture next to the yellow curtain. Chief Warrant Officer peeked behind the curtain for a second or two. The lighting was dark, and he found no person behind the curtain; instead he saw a bunch of blankets on the bed. Chief Warrant Officer then took off his rifle and set it down by his legs. He said it is something he does when he is at a friendly place as he does not want to talk with somebody with an assault rifle around his neck. It was a show of respect. His M4 rifle was semiautomatic and could fire on automatic also. The rifle was on safe mode.

After setting his gun down, the Chief Warrant Officer orientated himself toward the curtain of the room and the Ministry of Interior guys. He explained to them why he was there and what the FBI agents needed to do. As he began talking, within a second there was a loud scream of Allah u Akbar, Chief Warrant Officer's interpreter Gul screamed "Chief" really loudly, and at the same time Chief Warrant Officer saw Captain Snyder's eyes widen as if something was going to happen. When Chief

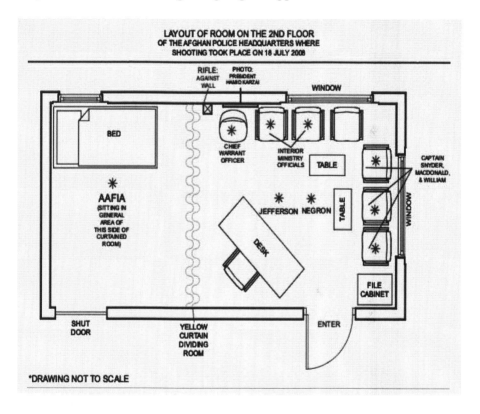

Warrant Officer looked to see what all the fuss was about, he saw a woman who had grabbed his M4 rifle and was pointing it toward the Chief Warrant Officer and others in the room. At this point, Chief Warrant Officer immediately went for his secondary weapon system, which was an M9 pistol, and fired two shots at her stomach, as she fired at the room. It was chaos in the room; there were people running out of the room as well as people running into the room.[123]

Interpreter Gul removed the yellow curtain completely, dived at the woman and pushed her against the wall. Interpreter Gul's right hand was on the barrel of her M4 rifle, and his left hand was on the buttstock of the rifle. He pushed the gun toward the ceiling because he was worried he might get shot.[124]

Agent Negron moved forward to secure her as well. As Agent Negron moved toward the woman, she started yelling, "I want to kill Americans. I want to kill Americans." She began to strike Agent Negron, attempting to bite and scratch him. Agent Negron fought back and hit her several times on the face and chest with a full fist. Eventually, he managed to grab her elbow as well as her arm and took her down toward the bed behind the curtain. Once they were on the floor she either fainted or faked she had fainted.[125] She was bleeding mildly from the gunshot wound on the left side of the stomach.[126] Agent Negron called the medic Card to come upstairs. He removed his shears from his vest and started to cut her clothes, in order to assist the woman. He also called Agent Jefferson to come in with the handcuffs so he could further restrain her. Agent Jefferson came in with the handcuffs, and both Agents handcuffed her. At this point the woman started to yell once again, "I want to kill Americans" and "Don't touch my blood, or you will die."[127] Medic Card lifted the woman's upper body and found two bullet holes in her lower abdomen. After checking the wounds, she realized she could not pack them. Therefore, she took the Kerlix and wrapped it around her abdomen to prevent any possible swelling that may occur from being shot in the abdomen. She did a quick check of her pulse to make sure she wasn't in any severe distress. Captain Snyder asked Card if they needed to call a medevac, she said the woman is stable and they can get her back to the FOB in the convoy. She said they just needed to go ahead and get her loaded up. Captain Snyder asked her if they needed a litter to be brought up. Card said no, because it would be incredibly difficult to get the litter down the stairs with the patient on it.[128] At that point, Chief

Warrant Officer looked out of the window and saw numerous members of the Afghan National Police orientating themselves, and their weapons towards the room.[129] They decided to move her out of the room with Agent Negron leading the way out of the door. As soon as Agent Negron stepped out of the door he immediately had several rifles pointed within inches of his face. He put his arm up in front of his face and started physically moving the rifles away from him and continued to go down the stairs.[130] Captain Snyder and other men picked the woman up and carried her downstairs. She was kicking her feet, nearly knocking Captain Snyder down the stairs.[131] There were also a large number of Afghan National Police cops standing at the ANP compound in an aggressive posture, pointing their guns at them.[132] When finally Captain Snyder and other gentlemen got her outside of the ANP building, they laid her down on the ground.[133] They brought the stretcher from one of the Humvee's and placed the woman on the stretcher while she continued to fight. Pat MacDonald and Captain Snyder attempted to pick up the stretcher. Pat was able to pick one side of the stretcher, but Captain Snyder couldn't hold the woman's ankles to stop her from kicking him. Sergeant Williams moved in to grab one ankle and one side of the stretcher. Captain Snyder grabbed the other side. They picked her up, and loaded her up into one of the Humvee's and brought her back to FOB, Ghazni.[134] There were some questions by counterterrorism representatives to Captain Snyder regarding what they were doing. Captain Snyder told them she was injured and they have to take her back. He said to meet them at FOB Ghazni where they could work out the details for detention.[135]

The woman was taken directly to the medical unit in FOB Ghazni. When Dawn Card arrived at the medical unit, she put down her gear and went to the unit trauma tables. The woman didn't want them to treat her. She wanted them to let her die, but they continued to treat her. Dawn Card provided a secure airway, gave her oxygen and checked her pupils and neck. The other members of the team worked on the rest of her, making sure there were no broken bones or excess bleeding. The team rechecked the bandage done by Medic Card.[136] FBI agents Negron and Jefferson stood outside the medical unit and later Governor Usman, and two Interior Ministry personnel came and joined them outside. Agents Negron and Jefferson were told the woman needed additional surgical care; therefore, she had to be flown to a better surgical medical unit. Once she became stable, both FBI agents and Sergeant Williams flew with her to Orgun-E on a Black Hawk helicopter. They transported the woman purse with them on the helicopter to Orgun-E. She had surgery at Orgun-E, and once she got stable Agent Negron took a picture of her which he wanted to e-mail to his senior to see if she was the woman the FBI was interested in. Then they left Orgun-E and took the woman to Bagram Airfield. Once they landed at Bagram Airfield, the woman was taken to the Craig Joint Hospital, and the woman's purse was handed over to the FBI heads.[137]

On July 19, 2008, the woman started receiving medical care at Bagram Medical facility. The FBI appointed a number of its Special Agents, who were responsible for security detail regarding her, to make sure she didn't escape or harm any of the medical providers. The Special Agents were on 12-hours shifts with at least two agents per shift to make sure she didn't do anything. There was also military police.[138] She also had soft hospital restraints. They were not handcuffs but were almost like terry cloth or felt with padding around her wrists and ankles attached to a strap and each strap was attached to the portion of the bed. She was given enough flexibility or enough leeway with each of the restraints so she could take care of her needs if she needed to read, if she needed to drink or if she needed to wash. But they situated them in a way so she wouldn't be able to get up or pose a threat to any of the medical workers or leave the room.[139]

Once a subject is brought into the FBI's custody specifically if they have been injured and they were in the hospital, it is the FBI's job to make sure of the person's safety and the safety of the others so they have to have 24-hour security.[140]

Special Agent Angela Sercer was called to the Medical Facility to take fingerprints of the woman so they could be processed to gain her full identity and also to conduct an interview. By this time, it was confirmed this detainee was Dr. Aafia Siddiqui, and the purpose of conducting interviews was to gather intelligence, related to the investigation which had been opened in the United States before her return to Pakistan in 2002. Dr. Aafia stayed at Bagram Medical Facility till July 4, 2008, and Agent Angela Sercer spoke with Dr. Aafia daily and recorded all of it in FD302, an official report regarding the interviews.[141] Angela Sercer described how Dr. Aafia's mental state varied. She said Dr. Aafia was much more distraught in the beginning, but later on she was more actively talking and smiling. She further said at times she enjoyed discussions with Angela Sercer and sometimes she was not interested in talking.[142]

Dr. Aafia, during her conversations with Angela Sercer, talked about her whereabouts during the four or five years before her arrest in Ghazni. Dr. Aafia shared she was in hiding and would move from place to place, and at one point she got married so her name would be changed and she could have a different name. She knew she was wanted for questioning by the US government, especially the FBI.[143]

Dr. Aafia said she had documents and other items in her possession when she was arrested in Ghazni. When she was confronted with those documents by Angela Sercer, she recognized some as possibly handwritten by her. Certain parts of the documents she recognized she had handwritten, other parts she didn't recognize and didn't declare were actually her handwritten notes. She said she had been conducting research on ways to protect the people of Pakistan.[144]

Dr. Aafia did ask Angela Sercer questions about possible criminal penalties for attempted murder and if the death penalty was a possibility for attempted murder. She also asked what would happen if somebody was accused of shooting people, didn't actually do it, but they actually got shot themselves. She also said spewing bullets at US soldiers was a bad thing.[145]

On July 21, 2008, Special Agent Bruce Kamerman was appointed to Dr. Aafia's room at Bagram Medical Facility for security on a shift basis. Dr. Aafia engaged Agent Bruce in conversations from July 21 to July 24, 2008. He initially noted down the details in a notebook and then later started recording them in an FD302 as he realized they were significant statements of an incriminating nature. Dr. Aafia told Agent Bruce she had taken a pistol shooting class while she was attending MIT. Agent Bruce then asked her follow-up questions on whether she had ever shot a rifle. She told him she had never seen, handled or fired a rifle. He further asked Dr. Aafia if she had ever fired a military M16 or M4 to which she replied that she had not. She also said she was not familiar with the function of safety on a military weapon such as an M16 or M4. Dr. Aafia also voluntarily told Bruce that on the day of the shooting she had picked up the rifle because she wanted to scare the men so she could escape.[146]

THE COUNTER VERSION OF THE CASE THROUGH DR. AAFIA SIDDIQUI'S TESTIMONY

Dr. Aafia Siddiqui said she was not afraid of speaking the truth, and something unusual did occur on July 18, 2008. Due to that incident she believed she was being put to trial. She said she had a personal dilemma, and this is what she has said several times about boycotting this trial. She has not been going into details about it all either. She feels by talking about this incident, she will be considered a liar. However, she wants to speak the truth.[147]

Dr. Aafia's first memory of July 18, 2008, was like every other day; concerned about her missing two or three children. Dr. Aafia always began her day worrying about her children.[148]

On July 17, 2008, night time, Americans came to check her at ANP police headquarters. Some were in uniform, and some were not. Some of them were immodest and behaved badly, even beating her up. Then Indians came, too. She begged the Afghans to keep her because they let her cover. She kept asking them nicely all night and all morning not to hand her over.[149] She said Afghans were not interested in being immodest or in torturing her. The Afghans said they wouldn't hand her over, but she wasn't convinced as she had been subjected to too many lies.[150]

On July 18, 2008, there was a press conference in the room with a lot of people coming into the room. She didn't want to deal with the media and didn't talk to any media person. She just kept her head down with her head covering all the way down. She didn't like to be photographed in the press. The Press Conference was in a room in the big prison building, and it was not the prison where she was kept the night before. She didn't morally agree she was part of any event which happened in that room on July 18, 2008, afternoon. Dr. Aafia agreed she was sitting on the bed in the room as she was tied up and had no choice. At one point her hands and feet were extremely swollen and blue, and she told the Afghans if they didn't untie her, they would have to feed her with a spoon for the rest of her life because she would lose her hands for good. They took her handcuffs off because they didn't want her to lose her hands. There was a curtain dividing the room, and she was behind the curtain. She heard some American and Afghan voices coming in the room, but because she was behind the curtain, she couldn't see what was going on. She understood at the time they wanted to take her away and she was very afraid because she didn't want to be thrown in another secret prison. She was very confused and frightened and wanted to get out. She got up from the bed and wanted to see what was going on. She knew it was stupid, but she thought when you were in a situation like this, and you knew you would be thrown in a secret prison, you must try to do anything to get away because nobody wanted to risk being taken to secret prison.[151]

When she moved toward the curtain, she found a gap on the edge. She didn't know how much of a gap it was, but she wanted to peek from there to see if she could get out. She thought if there was any room among or behind the people or maybe if they were busy talking, she could sit down and quietly sneak out. This was all going through her mind, and that was her intent when she moved toward the curtain. The next thing she knew was how somebody saw her and said something. A guy standing right at the opposite end of the room saw her and shot her. She was shocked. Then another set of people came and shot her and then she passed out. She was laid on the bed, and then some people with American voices came close which she could tell were soldiers and were saying "we are taking this B with us." She used the word B because she didn't like to use bad words. She passed out as she can't deal with blood which is why she couldn't become a medical doctor. Then they picked her up and threw her on the floor. She tried to resist, but she passed out again. The next thing she remembered being taken away. The person who shot her and the person who saw her being shot, said excitedly something like she's either free or lose.[152]

At times she remembered hearing things, but she had no power to move her body. She also remembered definitely whoever was with her through the journey. Dr. Aafia remembered the helicopter ride and the stretcher. She remembered they were putting her on some vehicle from a stretcher. She was conscious. One person was very concerned about two things. First when she was screaming and second when she experienced excruciating pain. Then before she passed out, another person said "Oh, my God she is going to die. A couple of us are going to lose our jobs." Both were very concerned about losing their jobs thinking they just had a few more hours of work saying something like "Oh no she's gone." She remembered during the helicopter ride she could not breathe again; there was something bottle like, and she saw blood bags going in her. It was against her will. She told whoever was there that blood transfusion is against her will and to get the bags off from her or if she ever got out, she would sue them. When she said that, the person laughed, and then somebody else laughed. They didn't take off the blood bag. Then she remembered the operating theater. She couldn't open her eyes, but she was conscious enough to hear something about X-rays. The next was the hospital in Bagram.[153]

On July 18, 2008, she didn't pick up any M4 rifle and didn't aim at anybody. She thought it was such a big joke that sometimes she was forced to smile under her scarf. She didn't think any of the American soldiers would be so irresponsible as to leave a gun lying around in a room full of people so that a detainee could walk up and operate it so fast when that detainee had never in her life seen an M4. In fact, she said in her conscious recollection she had seen an M4 rifle for the first time in the court. All the time she was wondering what an M4 rifle looked like. She recalled asking somebody if it was a pistol or one of the bigger rifles. She said it was because they shot her and now they are trying to cover it all up. She said she would never take revenge on anybody. Dr. Aafia shared she was making a public announcement about how she had forgiven them for doing that.[154]

On July 17, 2008, she was with a boy in Ghazni. About whether she was with her son or not, she said, "Um I don't know." She couldn't swear under oath to that. She said the reason she couldn't swear was because her son was missing for a long time and she hadn't seen him. It could have been her son, but she would never testify under oath on that. She said she takes the oath seriously. She said she was just not going to go into that question as it was not relevant. Dr. Aafia, said there was a boy with her, but she was in a daze at that time. If you ask a dazed person of what they thought at that time she was not sure if that was valid. Dr. Aafia also said she couldn't testify whether she had a number of documents in her possession that day because she was in a daze. She didn't check her bags. She didn't prepare them. It wasn't her stuff; the bag was given to her. She didn't go through each and everything in it on that day. She didn't know what was put in it. Dr. Siddiqui didn't want to lie, and she didn't want to testify on that. Some documents could possibly be in her handwriting as the stuff had been copied from a magazine and she couldn't testify on that because she didn't remember the words. She said she hadn't written the construction of the dirty bomb on the documents, and we had to understand that if a person is in secret prison, and their kids were tortured in front of them, they don't know how to do things they are asked to do. The worst they could do is copy something from a magazine. She didn't know how to make a dirty bomb. She testified she didn't have a clue. She was not even familiar with firearms. These documents were not her doing. The purse was given to her. She didn't know what was put in it; she didn't know that. She didn't even draw the pictures in the documents. Dr. Aafia shared she wasn't even a good artist. She couldn't draw a hand, and there were hands on documents.[155]

At MIT she probably could have taken pistol safety course as part of her physical education course. She remembered everybody used to take it. She didn't take any pistol course at the Braintree Rifle & Pistol Club, Boston while at MIT. She wasn't aware on July 18, 2008, that Americans wanted to question her. Americans wanted to have a talk, and her concern was about being transferred back to some kind of secret prison. She didn't think she was aware of them wanting to question her. She didn't see why they would want to question her. She said the Americans didn't want to question her since 2002.[156]

She said "God cured me, God cured me. Thank you." Americans did give her treatment. A nurse named Erica in Bagram Hospital Staff was nice to her and she appreciated that. She said if she ever wrote a book, she would mention her name. But she didn't think she was writing a book, so she was mentioning her name still. Her head hurt; she couldn't sleep for months on one side of her head. Dr. Aafia was sure that could lead to permanent brain damage because she passed out after being thrown. She couldn't move her back. She was covered from head to toe with bruises. Her wrist was swollen.[157]

She could recall her time when she was at the Craig Joint Theater Hospital in Bagram, Afghanistan. She said there were tubes everywhere. She couldn't move, she remembered. She couldn't move at all. They tried to do something with her thumb; she didn't know what. She had an IV in her arm. She had undergone major abdominal surgery to remove bullets from her abdomen. Dr. Aafia was sure she was given pain killers, but she didn't know which ones they were giving her. She was not told she might have been given morphine, but she believed they must have given her something because of what it did to her thinking. She meant, she could tell she was on drugs. Dr. Aafia remembered Ibuprofen. She didn't remember Fentanyl, but she was never told what they were giving her unless she asked. Haldon rang a bell, but she was still not sure. She was restrained to the bed, all four limbs tied; hands to the side and the feet, depending on who would put her cuffs on. She could never bring her feet together, and it was very uncomfortable. She was unable to reach anywhere; not even up to her mouth to eat.[158]

At no point did any person come to her room identifying himself to her as an agent of the Federal Bureau of Investigation, however, with just one exception which occurred only a day or two before she was taken out of the hospital. The rest of them wore something around their necks sometimes, not all of them, but what they wore was always turned. It was their standard practice. Any staff that came removed their badges before coming or flipped them. Everybody would wear some type of identification. Even the medical staff so she wasn't surprised about that. The only person who identified himself was Mr. Hurley, who was in court earlier, and he just told her his name and showed her his ID. He told her he was with the FBI and she didn't need to speak with him and how he would not ask her anything. He was a guard. He sat down and didn't ask anything. She didn't talk to him other than she would like to make peace. But other than that nobody introduced themselves, until Mehtab came and they were taking her. Agent Bruce did threaten her. He was very immodest, and his attitude was purely psychological emotional torture. She had to ask Agent Angela Sercer to remove him from having anything to do with her and to never have him in her room. When nurses used to come to dress her wounds, he would like to stand and watch. If she went to the bathroom, he would be at the door. As she couldn't walk due to the operation female guards had to take her to the bathroom, and he was always with the guards trying to say he was protecting the guards from her. He would instruct them to make her restraints tighter and filling the female guards with hate by saying how horrible she was. He told lies of all sorts. Even while talking, he would not be the person she would voluntarily ever agree to talk to. "Right now he is lying in the court." There was a lot more she could tell about what Agent Bruce did to her before she came to Bagram. He intimidated her many times. Many times Agent Sercer and Bruce threatened her that if she didn't speak to them, she would be taken somewhere else. She didn't remember the exact words, but in so many words saying that if you don't talk to them, you will be transferred to the group of bad boys. Dr. Aafia had been in a group of bad boys, and she didn't want to go to them again. She couldn't go to the bathroom without the permission of Agent Sercer and Bruce. She wasn't even in control when she had to eat. Bruce didn't spend a lot of time to her; he used to come in at nights when he wasn't supposed to. He would impose himself in her room and spend the whole night in the room. She couldn't sleep. She couldn't feel comfortable lying down so she would sit up in bed pretending to read. She was very sleep deprived. When she couldn't take that anymore, she talked to Agent Sercer, who said he shouldn't be coming in her room. He has nothing to do with her. She wasn't pleased with that. Agent Sercer never identified herself as an FBI agent, but she was a nice person.[159]

Dr. Aafia did give the phone number of her family to Craig Joint Theater Hospital staff; in fact, they had her family number. She never got to speak to her family. She never received any visit from anyone from the Pakistani government while at Craig Joint Hospital. Nobody ever came to her and explained her rights under the Geneva Convention. It was like she had no rights. She had been tortured at the secret prison before, and when she was at the Bagram Craig Joint Theater Hospital, she was afraid the same was going to happen to her again. She was afraid they would hand her over to someone else, but this time it was different from her past experiences in the secret prison. She kept asking them where her children were all the time, and they kept asking her where they were.[160]

On occasion, she did talk to Agent Sercer about her family and educational background. She even provided her home address and telephone number to Agent Sercer. Agent Sercer did bring photographs to her to recognize certain people, but she was very concerned about her children and their safety and that was on her mind pretty much. She wasn't eating. They were trying to make her eat. She couldn't eat because she couldn't digest the food. It gave her incredible pain to take one or more morsels. They were more concerned she was going to starve and die so, therefore, they had to feed her rather than denying her food. Mr. Hudson didn't want to take care of her, and he was not nice.[161] She told Agent Hurley that instead of sending her over to the US, she could help the US end the war and bring peace. She would like to do that, and if Hurley was serious then he should convey this to his boss.[162]

Dr. Aafia never said she picked up the rifle on July 18, 2008. She never asked Sercer hypothetically what a person would be charged with if they were involved in an incident where a gun went off and then the person accused of shooting the weapon ended up being shot themselves. She never got a chance to speak to Sercer. If she knew Sercer was an FBI agent, she would have probably told Sercer her kids were being held, and she was under threat if she didn't say what she had been told to say hundreds of times or if she messed up, they would kill her daughter, rape her daughter, kill her, and how one baby was already gone. Now, she understood how they set up and framed people. Now as they were using all of that there in that court, it confirmed what she had been saying all along that there was a group of people pretending to be Americans, doing bad things in the name of America and that is how they began wars, and that was why America couldn't get out of Afghanistan. That was why she could end the war because she knew what was going on. "When you know what the problem is, you can easily eliminate it, and that's the end of the war." That is why Dr. Aafia claimed one day to let her talk. But she was not given the opportunity by those people, the war makers.[163]

Chapter 5
Did Dr. Aafia Shoot An M4 Rifle?

*F*OR THOSE QUESTIONING THE EVENTS SUR-rounding the rifle shooting Dr. Aafia found herself in, in the previous chapter, I explained in detail the versions of both prosecution and Dr. Aafia regarding the shooting event which took place on July 18, 2008, in the room on the second floor of Afghan National Police headquarters, Ghazni.

Prosecution witnesses testified Dr. Aafia did grab Chief Warrant Officer's M4 rifle and shot at the room, whereas Dr. Aafia denied grabbing any M4 rifle and shooting at the room. In this chapter, I have discussed in detail the testimonies of FBI Agent Hurley, Physical Scientist Mr. Carlo J. Rosati, Mr. D.J. Fife, and Material Science and Metallurgy expert Mr. Bill Tobin.

Agent Hurley was assigned by the US government to investigate the shooting at the crime scene and collect forensic evidence. Mr. Carlo J. Rosati was contracted by the US government to do firearm examination, gunpowder residue examination and debris examination of the evidence. Mr. J.R. Fife was contracted by the US government to examine the items of evidence for latent fingerprints. Mr. Bill Tobin, retained by the defense, gave his expert opinion while reviewing the laboratory reports, some physical evidence, and witnesses' interviews. While reading these testimonies, the reader will, hopefully, be able to reach an informed opinion about whether Dr. Aafia shot from an M4 rifle or not.

The Chief Warrant Officer said Dr. Aafia grabbed his M4 rifle and pointed it at him and others in the room and then she fired at the room.[164] Captain Snyder said he saw Dr. Aafia kneeling on the bed that was beyond the curtain, holding an M4 rifle, and attempting to shoulder it and pointing it at him. She fired at least three shots.[165] Agent Negron said Dr. Aafia was holding M4 rifle with one hand on the barrel and her other hand was on the trigger. She began to fire two to three shots into the room.[166] Interpreter Gul said he saw Dr. Aafia holding a rifle, pointing it at the direction of the Chief Warrant Officer, two FBI agents and the ministry of interior representatives, and made two shots.[167]

Dawn Card said she saw Dr. Aafia holding the M4 rifle and she fired it. Card could see the bullets going by, they hit the wall, and the wall flaked off. Pieces of the wall were flying in front of her.[168] Interpreter Amin saw Dr. Aafia was holding M4 rifle and shouting "get the fuck out of here." He heard the one shot and he didn't know where exactly it hit because he thinks the gun barrel was toward ceiling, so maybe somewhere on top of the wall or the ceiling somewhere.[169]

Dr. Aafia said she never picked up the M4 rifle and aimed it at any American soldiers or even fired.[170] Bashir, an Afghan eyewitness, said he heard gunshots were fired in the room. He didn't see Dr. Aafia fire any of the shots.[171]

Late night on July 18, 2008, FBI Agent Hurley and Special Agent Michael Moorehead were assigned by the US government to investigate the shooting which occurred at the ANP headquarters, Ghazni. Both were told to make plans to deploy to that area and get down there and find out what happened as soon as possible. When Dr. Aafia arrived at Bagram hospital at early morning of July 19, 2008, both agents went to the hospital and obtained her fingerprints, blood and hair samples but did not take her DNA samples. They also didn't collect Dr. Aafia's incident clothing as a piece of evidence. They interviewed one of the doctors at the hospital and then interviewed Agent Jefferson, Agent Erik Negron, Staff Sergeant Williams, Captain Snyder, Army Medic Card, Chief Warrant officer, John Kendall, interpreters Ahmed Gul, and some other person who were either present or had knowledge of what had happened. They reached Ghazni on July 22, 2008, and on July 24, 2008, for the first time, they visited the crime scene.[172]

When they got into the room, they had everyone walk out of there and made sure no one was present. They did a visual inspection, looking for anything which was readily apparent. They took a video of the room with a small digital camera. Furthermore, they took still photographs of the room and any item they found in it. They measured the room and prepared a very rough sketch.[173]

They took photographs of the walls and looked for areas with damage possibly caused by a gunshot or a bullet. They found two holes on the wall which was immediately to the right as one entered the main door of the room, which they thought possibly to be gunshot damage. One of these two holes was present at 7-feet and five inches if you measured from the floor up, and the other hole was 7-feet and 7 inches from the floor up; close to the ceiling. Toward the back of the room, they discovered two additional holes in the wall which indicated possible gunshot damage. They also found one hole in the ceiling but when Agent Hurley looked at it closely it had a circular pattern around it as if a light fixture or maybe a fan or something similar had been up around it at some point. So, it didn't appear to be a gunshot. So, during the visual inspection of the room, they found in total four holes on the walls which they possibly thought were due to gunshot damage. It was impossible for them to determine definitively the damage to the walls was in fact caused by the gunshots, unless they gathered that evidence and sent it back to the lab.[174]

To determine if there was a bullet or any other item which caused these holes they tried to excavate one of the holes, but the wall began to crumble. It was a masonry material; with a tough exterior as well as having dust. As they were excavating, one of the special forces folks who was with them advised them not to excavate the wall any further, as it was an Afghan Police station and not US property. The Americans had no permission to destroy or mess up Afghan property. They did a visual inspection of the floor with flashlights looking for any bullets, casings, bullet fragments, etc. They did a quick walk around the room as well as a quick check underneath the furniture. They found a bullet which appeared to be from an M9 firearm.[175] They also collected the incident M4 rifle with the docter sight but without its flashlight and laser equipment, and an M9 semiautomatic pistol from Captain Kendall.[176]

On August 25, 2008, both agents went back to the crime scene for a more thorough investigation. They brought the ladder this time and also some hand tools. They brought in some fairly heavy picks and an ax as well as some things of that nature to use if they had to chop out a portion of the wall. They had knives and other cutting instruments with them. They started inspecting the room furniture first for any possible damage from a gunshot. Then, they moved the room furniture to one side (of the room) and did a comprehensive look of the floor. They also pulled the carpet back and examined the floor. They found a single nine millimeter cartridge on the floor. Throughout the rest of the day, during the inspection, they didn't find any more cartridges or bullets in the room. Out of the four holes in the walls, this time both agents were more focused on two holes which were immediately to the right as one entered the door of the room. They found these two holes the most probable of being from gunshot damage. They started to excavate the two holes (only), and the moment they started excavating, the wall began to crumble again, but they dug all the way through to the outside wall and to the outside of the building. During the excavation of the holes, they didn't find any apparent bullets or bullet fragments. Agent Hurley then went up to the roof and looked down to see if there was any penetration; he didn't find anything. They made a bag of about 25 or 30 pounds of debris that was dug out of the holes in the wall for evidence. Then they took the yellow curtain off, the one which was dividing the room to test for gunshot or gunpowder residue evidence. Mr. Janagha who worked for the Afghan National Police station gave them another nine-millimeter cartridge. He found it in the room 20 to 30 minutes after the shooting incident.[177] During the investigation of the crime scene, both agents couldn't find any evidence of an M4 bullet in the entire crime scene neither M4 bullet fragments in the holes.[178]

Carlo J. Rosati who was a physical scientist, firearm and toolmark examiner, for the Federal Bureau of Investigation was contacted by the United States of America government to conduct firearm examinations, and gunshot residue examinations on evidence found during the investigation of the crime scene.[179] He examined whether a nine-millimeter bullet found in the room was fired from the incident M9 pistol. He test-fired the M9 pistol and then upon examination he rendered an opinion that a nine-millimeter bullet was fired from the incident M9 pistol. Furthermore, he also compared the two crime scene cartridge cases with the test-fired cartridges of the incident M9 pistol, and concluded the cartridges cases were from the same M9 pistol. He also examined the incident M4 rifle and test fired it in the FBI laboratory, but he was not given any bullets, bullet fragments, or cartridge cases to compare to that firearm. He did gunshot residue examination on the docter sight and didn't find any gunshot or gunpowder residue on it. Rosati didn't do any further chemical examination of it. He did a gunshot or gunpowder residue examination on the yellow curtain to check for any gunshot residue on it. As part of the examination first, he looked for any bullet hole present in the curtain, which he couldn't find. Then he did a macroscopic examination of the curtain while holding it up against the light and didn't find any unburned or partially burned gunshot or gunpowder residue. He concluded he found no gunpowder residue on the curtain from the M9 pistol and the M4 Rifle.[180] He examined the bag of debris in the laboratory to find any bullet or bullet fragments in the debris. During the examination he began by looking for any large bullet fragments macroscopically, and then he did a microscopic examination, but didn't find anything. He then proceeded to do an examination using a metal detector but still didn't find any bullet or bullet fragment in the debris.[181]

Mr. Rosati was also shown not the highest quality photographs of two holes on the wall to find the bullet impacts. This led to him not being able to examine precisely because of the quality of the images. Then he was shown the video of the wall, too, but even then he couldn't examine the bullet impacts on the wall due to quality of the video.[182]

D.J. Fife who was a physical scientist and forensic examiner worked in the FBI latent print operation unit. His work at the laboratory was to examine the items of evidence for latent prints and fingerprints work. Mr. Fife was contacted by the United States of America government to get latent fingerprints of value from the M4 rifle and a sight. He examined the M4 rifle and sight for the latent fingerprint of value. He didn't recover any latent fingerprints of value from anybody on them. He examined these items in an examination room where he had large magnifiers. Mr. Fife put two lights on the items and examined every surface by using the magnifier. Then he took both in the light source room and did a full examination while using a laser light and ultraviolet light. After then he performed a super glue fuming method, but didn't find any latent fingerprint of value. He also tried examining both by using a piece of equipment called RUVIS, which stands for Reflected Ultraviolet Imaging System, but still didn't find any latent fingerprints of value on them. The last thing he tried was he applied white fingerprint powder on items, but still failed to see any latent fingerprint on them.[183]

Mr. Bill Tobin, an expert in material science and metallurgy, was retained by the defense. He previously worked in the FBI lab as a forensic metallurgist and retired as a de facto chief forensic metallurgist. He reviewed numerous case materials which included FBI laboratory reports.

He also examined some physical evidence involved in the case and did review some witnesses' interviews. Mr. Tobin gave his expert opinion that the two holes on the wall which were considered to be gunshot damage were not marks from a high-velocity bullet fired from an M4 rifle. He said he has reached an opinion to a degree of scientific certainty. In reaching this decision, he said he considered the manufacturing and construction characteristics of the bullet. He also considered the amount of kinetic energy (energy due to motion) the bullet had undergone for it to result in a state of rest due to the force of the wall upon it. He then considered the penetration mechanics, including the angle at which the bullet impacted the wall, as well as the uniaxial compressive strength of the concrete wall.[184]

He continued giving his expert while explaining the M4 rifle SS109 5.56-millimeter bullet has more than twice the gunpowder than the M9 pistol nine-millimeter bullet. He estimated 13 grains of powder in the nine-millimeter bullet and 28.8 grain in the SS109 5.56-millimeter bullet. Mr. Tobin said that for a nine millimeter, the pressure inside the barrel of the gun is typically 35,000 to 37,000 pounds per square inch whereas for an SS109 5.56 millimeter it is 56,000 pounds per square inch, which meant the pressure inside the M4 rifle is doubled. He found it strange how no fragments from the SS109 5.56 millimeter bullets have been recovered from the crime scene and especially from the holes in the wall. He also said the gunshot residue from a M4 rifle travels farther than the M9 pistol and there must have been some dispersion[185]. Therefore, he believed, from his scientific opinion, the two holes in the wall were not due to an M4 rifle firing SS109 5.56mm bullets.[186]

Chapter 6

Dr. Aafia And Her Mental Competency To Stand Trial

R. AAFIA'S MENTAL COMPETENCY TO stand trial was the core contention between the prosecution and defense attorneys before the trial hearings. The prosecution and defense attorneys retained their own mental health professionals to conduct additional psychiatric analysis and evaluation of Dr. Aafia. Here I have mentioned in detail the events which took place in court before the competency hearing, the mental health reports submitted by the retained psychiatrists, and finally what the court competency hearing concluded.

Dr. Aafia was arrested at 8:00 am, on August 04, 2008 in Afghanistan. On August 5, 2008, Dr. Aafia appeared before the Magistrate Court Judge Ronald L. Ellis in the Southern District of New York. The purpose of the proceeding was to inform Dr. Aafia of her rights and also to inform her about the charges against her. Judge Ellis explained to Dr. Aafia that 1) She had the right to remain silent. 2) She wasn't required to make any statement, even if she had made any statements to the authorities she did not need to make any further statements. 3) Anything she has said can be used against her. 4) She has the right to be released on bail either with conditions or without conditions pending trial. 5) She had the right to be represented by counsel during all court proceedings and during all questioning by the authorities. 6) If she could not afford an attorney, the court would appoint one to represent her.[187]

Dr. Aafia understood all the guidelines. She completed a financial affidavit and signed it. The financial affidavit indicated she had no assets, she was not employed, had no property and she had no income. The Court then appointed Attorney Elizabeth Fink to represent Dr. Aafia.

Elizabeth Fink was the CJA attorney on duty in the Magistrate Court and was appointed by the court. In the beginning, Dr. Aafia didn't understand the criminal complaint and the charges against her, but after the judge read them out to her, she understood. Attorney Fink explained to the judge that Dr. Aafia had been shot twice in her abdomen and was in pain as well as that Fink had looked at the wound dressing and how it was stained and oozing. Fink apprised the court that Dr. Aafia was not getting antibiotics or painkillers and she was totally dehydrated. She also explained Dr. Aafia was a devout Muslim and her religion must be respected during the trial. Fink notified the court that Dr. Aafia needed a special diet, i.e., a Halal diet. The judge said he would make a note that Dr. Aafia was suffering from a bullet wound and needed to be looked at for treatment.[188] Prosecution attorney Mr. LaVigne stated when Dr. Aafia left Afghanistan, she was accompanied by a physician who was on the plane with her until she landed in the United States and was there to provide medical care for her.[189]

On August 11, 2008, Fink appeared before Magistrate Court Judge Henry B. Pitman and introduced Gideon Oliver, Sarah Kunstler, and Daniel Meyers, who worked with her. Fink also introduced attorney Elaine Whitfield Sharp to the court. Elaine was representing the family of Dr. Aafia since 2003 in the USA. Fink requested the judge for a court order for pain medication for Dr. Aafia and her right to use a wheelchair. The judge asked Mr. LaVigne about the situation with respect to Dr. Aafia's medical care, and if she had seen a physician at the Metropolitan Detention Center, Brooklyn. Mr. LaVigne explained they had been in contact with the Bureau of Prison (BOP), and Dr. Aafia had seen a medical professional although Mr. LaVigne didn't believe he was an M.D. The judge asked whether there was any reason why a physician shouldn't see Dr. Aafia. Mr. LaVigne explained that according to their understanding, Dr. Aafia declined to be seen by a male medical doctor and no female medical doctor was working at BOP.[190]

Fink notified the court that on August 8, 2008, a counselor from Pakistan embassy in Washington, a High-level person from the Pakistan Consulate of New York and Gideon Oliver went to see Dr. Aafia at MDC Brooklyn. Oliver explained to the Pakistan authorities Dr. Aafia is in pain and she needed to see a doctor, and she would see a female doctor. Fink also stated Ms. Kunstler, who was in constant contact with the MDC and had spoken to MDC attorney Adam Johnson, was informed Dr. Aafia had not been seen by a doctor yet. Fink suggested Dr. Aafia needed to be taken out of BOP custody and put in a hospital.[191] The court asked Mr. LaVigne if there was any impediment to her being seen by a physician within the next 24 hours.[192]

Ms. Sharp, an expert on medical issues, addressed to the court that Dr. Aafia had been shot and there were gunshot wounds in her abdomen. Sharp said she saw a long line of stitches from Dr. Aafia's breastplate down to her belly button and it was about eight to ten inches of stitches on a very small woman. Sharp further added Dr. Aafia had lost part of her intestine and so digestion was an issue. She said Dr. Aafia reported some internal bleeding. Therefore, she needed to be seen by a physician. Furthermore, Dr. Aafia had not received any physical therapy, and she was in danger of tearing her abdominal stitching layer-by-layer by bending down and sitting up. Sharp suggested to the court that Dr. Aafia needed to be evaluated by an internist who can make referral to the general abdominal surgeon, who then might make a referral for a CT scan or an MRI of the area to rule out any serious bleeding which could lead to infection.[193] The court then directed that a medical doctor examined Dr. Aafia and not a physician assistant or a registered nurse, within 24 hours.[194]

On or around September 2, 2008, an indictment was filed against Dr. Aafia charging her with a number of counts, including 1- Attempted murder of United States nationals in violation of 18 U.S.C. section 2332(b)(1) and 3228; 2- Attempted murder of United States officers and employees in violation of 18 U.S.C. section 114(3) and 3238; 3- Armed assault against United States officers and employees in violation of 18 U.S.C. section 924(c)(1)(A)(iii), 924(c)(1)(B)(ii) and 3238; 4- Assault against United States officers and employees (Interpreter one) in violation of 18 U.S.C. section 111(a)(1) and 3238; 5- Assault against United States officers and employees (FBI special Agent one) in violation of 18 U.S.C. section 111((a)(1) and 3238; 6- Assault against United States officers and employees (U.S. Army officer Two) in violation of 18 U.S.C. Section 111(a)(1) and 3238. Each offence was alleged to have occurred on or around July 18, 2008, at an Afghan National Police compound in Ghazni, Afghanistan.[195]

By a letter dated September 03, 2008, Fink informed the court that when Dr. Aafia met with Pakistani authorities on August 08, 2008, she was handcuffed behind her back. She was made to walk from one side of the MDC building to another without her wheelchair, was strip-searched, and was placed in a cell separated from her visitors by bars covered by Plexiglas. Fink also explained that on August 9, 2008, she and her team were able to have a two-hour meeting with Dr. Aafia although they were continuously interrupted by people walking through that area. After their visit Dr. Aafia was strip searched again. Fink said after this visit Dr. Aafia refused all subsequent visits to avoid being subjected to strip searches. Fink also informed the court that Dr. Aafia had been evaluated to a limited extent by Psychological staff at MDC Brooklyn. The Psychological staff report revealed she had been crying in her cell neglecting her food tray and making bizarre requests, including a request the turkey from her meal tray be placed in a refrigerator so it could be sent to her son. Although Fink was able to get a psychologist, Dr. Antonia Cedrone, to examine Dr. Aafia on permission by Chief Magistrate Judge Pitman, but due to the MDC requirement Dr. Aafia be strip searched before seeing Dr. Cedrone, he couldn't visit Dr. Aafia to conduct an examination. On the request of Fink, Dr. Cedrone reviewed the psychological report prepared by the MDC staff and prepared an analysis report that Dr. Aafia's mental condition has deteriorated since her confinement at MDC.[196]

Fink further stated in the letter that Dr. Aafia was isolated entirely from her attorneys, psychological help and her family. She said Dr. Aafia was permitted one telephone call to her family every 30 days and one legal telephone call every two weeks. She also said Dr. Siddiqui didn't want to speak to her by telephone. Finally, Fink made an observation Dr. Aafia was not competent to participate in her own defense or to stand trial and required further evaluation including examination by medical professionals specializing in the treatment of torture victims and a course of treatment which could help her regain her mental health.[197]

On September 4, 2008, Judge Burman held a status conference in which Dr. Aafia indicated she doesn't want to appear, and she didn't appear. Judge Berman was ready for arraignment proceedings, but Dr. Aafia was not present in the court. Fink stressed there should be an arraignment for which either the court should go to the MDC or the court does it by video so Dr. Aafia was not strip searched.[198] Fink further added Dr. Aafia was unbelievably damaged and was in isolation. She said the only people Dr. Aafia talked to were jail prison officials. Fink thought some of them were FBI agents which Dr. Aafia was constantly looking to speak to. Fink also stated Dr. Aafia has extreme anxiety about her children and she knew one of them had been located. Judge Berman objected Fink and stated Psychological counseling was offered to Dr. Aafia at the MDC, but she declined. Judge Berman further added the court had already figured out ways to provide stabilization or psychological support to Aafia.[199]

Fink then brought the attention of the court to gynecological problems Dr. Aafia was facing, which could not be discussed in open court but they were enormously serious. She said these gynecological problems had been going on since she came to the US and those problems were mentioned in the incomplete medical reports received from Bagram.[200] Fink asked the court for an order that gynecological examination be conducted by a female doctor. The court said it found no problem with ordering that.[201] The court ordered a medical evaluation, including a gynecological examination of Dr. Aafia, be conducted by a female doctor.[202]

By a letter dated September 5, 2008, Prosecution attorney Mr. LaVigne informed the court that a female doctor from the Federal Correctional Center in Otisville traveled to the MDC and attempted to examine Dr. Aafia. The government had been advised that despite the female doctor's extensive efforts, Dr. Aafia refused to be examined by her.[203]

Then by a memo endorsement, dated September 8, 2008, the court directed the United States Bureau of Prisons (BOP) to perform a psychological exam at MDC of Dr. Aafia forthwith, and apprise the court and the attorneys of the results as soon as possible.[204] By an order dated September 9, 2008, the court directed the "psychological exam" ordered by the court on September 8, 2008 shall include a forensic evaluation to be conducted at the MDC.[205]

Through a letter dated September 10, 2008, the court was informed by BOP Warden Cameron Lindsay that MDC Psychiatrist Diane McLean M.D. performed a psychological examination of Dr. Aafia on September 9, 2008. The letter also indicated that Dr. McLean conducted the first psychiatric evaluation of Dr. Aafia on September 2, 2008 and reported she had a depressed mood, anxiety as well as ruminative thoughts concerning her son's welfare, and also seeing her daughter in her cell. She also reported that during the evaluation Dr. Aafia didn't cooperate with Dr. McLean at all and didn't wish to take any psychotropic medications stating it won't fix her problem. On the second psychiatric evaluation conducted by Dr. McLean on September 9, 2008, pursuant to the court order Dr. Aafia received an Axis I diagnosis of Depressive Type Psychosis. Dr. McLean said that during the interview Dr. Aafia spoke through the blanket she had placed over her body, including her face. She politely said she didn't wish to speak with a psychiatrist or psychologist. She also said she didn't wish to be medically examined stating "I am fine" and that "no one cares about me here." She didn't answer Dr. McLean's questions concerning sleep, appetite, and food intake. However, the log book indicates she slept and ate according to Ramadan Schedule.[206]

By a letter dated September 16, 2008, Fink wrote to the court of Dr. Aafia's present condition and the urgent need to treat her in a hospital setting. She added that since September 4, 2008, she had been researching the nature of Dr. Aafia's illness and treatment options in the New York City area. After speaking with a number of psychiatric professionals, unit managers, and hospital administrators, she believed the forensic unit at Elmhurst Hospital administered by the New York City Department of Corrections fulfills all the criteria for Dr. Aafia's treatment in a custodial setting. Fink also said she spoke on a call with Dr. Aafia for the first time since August 11, 2008. She said before this call, Ms. Kunstler was informed by Adam Johnson that Dr. Aafia was no longer accepting legal mail. However, when Dr. Aafia learned her letter and material concerned the release of her son to her family in Pakistan, she opened it, saw the pictures of the reunion and asked to speak to her. Dr. Aafia's torment and pain resonated through the call as she said she was plagued by visions (hallucinations) of her two younger children who appear in her cell.[207]

By letter dated September 19, 2008, the prosecution wrote to the court it believed a competency hearing and a complete psychiatric evaluation of Dr. Aafia is warranted. The government further added that under Section 4241, the courts are required to hold competency hearing only when there was a reasonable cause to believe that the defendant may presently be suffering from a mental disease or defect rendering them mentally incompetent to the extent that she is unable to understand the nature and consequences of the proceedings against her or to assist properly in her defense. The government explained that in the competency hearing, the court is required to satisfy the *Dusky test*, which was whether the defendant has (1) sufficient present ability to consult with his lawyer with a reasonable degree of rational understanding and (2) a rational as well as factual understanding of the proceeding against them.[208]

The government found complete Psychiatric Evaluation and a Competency hearing the best method to establish an adequate record for a competency determination under the present circumstances. The government also believed that apart from the MDC psychiatrist diagnosis, Dr. Aafia's mental health record was essentially barren with respect to competency. The government further explained that mental health professionals at the prison had little meaningful interaction with Dr. Aafia and treatment records many of which the court had seen were subject to varying interpretations. The government also said the court had no opportunity to observe Dr. Aafia and the defense counsel had no face-to-face contact with her; only minimal phone contact. Law enforcement personnel who spent more than 20 hours with Dr. Aafia on the flight from Afghanistan to the US and carried on a bit of a chit-chat with Dr. Aafia observed no sign of mental illness, in their lay opinion. For all of the foregoing reasons, the government respectfully requested the court to direct (1) A psychiatric examination of Dr. Aafia to be conducted over a 30-day period at a suitable facility to be determined by the Bureau of Prisons (2) Preparation of a psychiatric report and (3) To set a competency hearing at a date to be determined by the court.[209]

On September 23, 2008, the court held a further status conference to discuss the request letters submitted by both prosecution and defense attorneys. Dr. Aafia was not present in the court. Prosecution attorney Mr. Ruskin explained that the government had an opportunity to review some of the medical records and the records of the psychiatrists and psychologists at the MDC. The records showed Dr. Aafia herself was refusing to participate in any evaluation. She had conversations with the psychiatrists and psychologists but had not submitted to anything which could conceivably be considered an examination. The government notified the court the federal law statute provided the court with authority to order that a complete forensic psychiatric exam be conducted to determine Dr. Aafia's competence. The government further asked the court not only to order an examination but to order that a report be prepared by the psychiatrists who conduct that examination and that a hearing be held before the court to determine Dr. Aafia's competency.[210]

On the other hand, Fink argued that Dr. Aafia was not competent. She explained that Dr. Aafia was sitting in a cell screaming and refusing to come out. Fink said Dr. Aafia was crazy and she couldn't make a mental determination. She was just not letting anybody touch her because she was in total psychological pain. Therefore, Dr. Aafia needed treatment and not an evaluation which could only happen at Elmhurst Hospital.[211]

After hearing both prosecution and defense attorneys, Judge Berman reminded the attorneys of the BOP Warden Cameron Lindsay letter to the court dated September 10, 2008, which stated that the MDC had offered assistance, both psychological and medical, which Dr. Aafia refused. He said the letter also stated that the MDC did what they described as intake screening and mental status monitoring throughout August and September of 2008. Judge Berman then made his findings, based on the records of the court proceedings and the submissions of the attorneys, that Dr. Aafia's non-appearance at the status conference hearing was voluntary and in such circumstances the court under the Federal Rule of Criminal Procedure 11(A)(4) is directed to enter *"a not guilty plea"* for Dr. Aafia who refused to enter a plea. Fink added she has no objection to the court entering a plea of not guilty but, she really had an objection to the finding that Dr. Aafia had knowingly, willingly and with competency absented herself. Fink shared a September 12, 2008 incident with the court when the psychologist Diana Guerrero Comb went to see Dr. Aafia at the MDC. Diana said that after a few minutes in the room, Dr. Aafia went to the door visibly crying and upset, and told Diana she could not go to the court because the video that was taken of her during the medical examination on September 9, 2008, was going to be or was already placed on the internet for everyone to watch. Dr. Aafia stated if she went to court, she would be ashamed because the people in the court had already seen the video of her naked on the internet.[212]

Upon the perusal of the record of the proceedings, including prior conferences, submissions of counsel, court orders, and attorneys request for a competency determination, and the court having considered various options proposed by attorneys, the court on October 01 2008, ordered that a hearing will be conducted to determine whether Dr. Aafia is medically fit and mentally competent to understand the nature and consequences of the proceedings against her or to assist properly in her defense, pursuant to 18 U.S.C §§ 4241(b) and (c), on or before December 17, 2008 at 10:00 a.m.The court further ordered that prior to the hearing, Dr. Aafia's complete medical assessment (and appropriate medical treatment) at a United States Bureau of Prisons medical facility shall be conducted and shall also include a psychiatric and/or psychological examination (and appropriate mental health treatment) for a period of 30-days, in order to evaluate whether Dr. Aafia is medically fit and mentally competent to stand trial, i.e., to understand the nature and consequences of the proceeding against her and to assist properly in her defense and at trial, pursuant to 18 U.S.C. §§ 4241 (b) and 4247(b), and the court further ordered that the facility at which Dr. Aafia is treated and evaluated shall be the one that has the resources to treat Dr. Aafia medical and psychological needs.[213]

Pursuant to the Court's Order, dated October 1, 2008, Dr. Aafia was transferred to the Federal Medical Center (FMC) Carswell in Fort Worth, Texas on October 2, 2008.[214]

In reply to the court order dated October 1, 2008, the court received a psychological evaluation report, dated November 6, 2008, by Leslie Powers, Ph.D., forensic psychologist, United States Department of Justice,

Federal Bureau of Prisons, Federal Medical Center Carswell. Dr. Powers and the members of the forensic team, as well as the correctional and medical staff, had the opportunity to observe Dr. Aafia's behavior during the course of the evaluation. The team also observed Dr. Aafia's telephone calls to her brother, Muhammad Siddiqui, which were monitored.

The evaluation report stated that when Dr. Aafia arrived at FMC Carswell, she refused to submit to the visual search process, which involved disrobing, as required by the Bureau of Prisons policy. Then a Use of Force team was gathered, and a video camera was brought in for determination. When Dr. Aafia saw the video camera, she began to cry and scream loudly, stating the camera had already killed her once. Eventually, she agreed to participate in the search voluntarily as long as a female officer did it and no video camera was used. There were some concerns about her eating habits when she arrived at Carswell because she had refused several meals at the MDC and had an extremely thin appearance. When asked about her eating, she stated she was not refusing to eat, but instead, she simply had no appetite. She spent most of the time in her room and isolated herself from the rest of the patients. Although she asked for a copy of the Quran, she stated she was unable to read it very well. Due to her religious affiliation, she requested a common tray, which was prepared following the dietary requirements of the Muslim religion. When the first time the food tray was served to her, she reported that her food had a "bitter taste" and reported experiencing severe abdominal pains immediately after eating one or two bites. She also described experiencing auditory hallucinations during her evaluation period. Dr. Aafia told several staff members she had seen her baby downstairs and requested to be able to go see him. Some days she reported her baby had walked into her room to see her. When describing this incident, she began to cry and stated, "He was so thin, and I don't think they are feeding him." She also reported this to other patients in her unit as well as her brother and a representative from the Pakistani Consulate. During her stay at FMC Carswell, she refused to consider any psychotropic medication and had been inconsistent in agreeing to participate in routine medical care. She stated that the court had already sentenced her to death and killed her so she didn't believe she would be going back to court for an additional hearing. She displayed a significant distrust of her attorneys, medical personnel, court officials, and psychological examiners.

In summary, Dr. Powers shared an opinion that Dr. Aafia was incompetent to proceed at this time as a result of her mental illness. He said Dr. Aafia was diagnosed with Major Depressive Disorder Severe with Mood Congruent Psychotic Features based on her depressive symptomology, her disinterest in participating in activities, and her self-report of appetite, sleep and concentration difficulties. Dr. Powers further opinioned that, there is a probability psychotropic medication would address the depression and psychotic symptoms that affect her competency, but they were unable to proceed with the treatment as a result of Dr. Aafia's refusal to take medication. Without such medication, Dr. Aafia would likely remain incompetent to stand for trial.[215]

After that, both government and defense attorney retained their own (respective) mental health professionals to conduct additional psychiatric analysis and evaluations of Dr. Aafia. On retention of mental health professionals by both parties, the court on December 23, 2008, made the following directions that (1) The Mental Health Professionals shall be permitted access to FMC Carswell and the Metropolitan Detention Center in Brooklyn, New York ("MDC Brooklyn) for purposes of conducting the Evaluations (2) The Mental Health Professionals shall be permitted to interview Dr. Aafia for purposes of the Evaluations (3) The Mental Health Professionals shall be permitted to interview any other individuals at FMC Carswell and MDC Brooklyn relating to the competence and mental health treatment of Dr. Aafia for purposes of the Evaluations (4) The Mental Health Professionals shall be permitted to review, inspect, and/ or copy any documentation or information at FMC Carswell and MDC Brooklyn relating to the competence of Dr. Aafia, for purposes of conducting the Evaluations (5) The Mental Health Professionals are permitted to discuss the Evaluations with the Government, the Court, defense counsel, and treating or examining psychiatrists, psychologists, or mental health staff at FMC Carswell and MDC Brooklyn.[216]

By a letter dated March 18, 2009, the prosecution retained two psychiatrists, Gregory B. Saathoff & Sally C, Johnson, who submitted their separate evaluation reports to the court on Dr. Aafia's competency to stand trial. The reports indicated that both psychiatrists reviewed a wealth of information including available medical records and reports of interviews of Dr. Aafia. Also, the psychiatrists conducted over eighty interviews including, interviews of Dr. Aafia herself, certain Bureau of Prisons mental health professionals and staff member who treated and observed Dr. Aafia and various federal agents who interviewed and observed Dr. Aafia.

Based on available information, both psychiatrists concluded Dr. Aafia is competent to stand trial. Especially one psychiatrist who concluded that Dr. Aafia is medically fit to stand trial as her medical problems have been treated and stabilized. He said Dr. Aafia is not presently suffering from a mental disease or defect rendering her mentally incompetent to the extent she is unable to understand the nature and consequences of the proceedings or to assist properly with her defense. He further said Dr. Aafia has a rational and factual understanding of the proceedings against her and is able to assist her attorneys with a reasonable degree of rational understanding should she choose to do so. He said Dr. Aafia's 'lack of co-operation' in the evaluation process 'is volitional and not a symptom of mental illness' and rather it is consistent with 'malingering.'[217]

Detailed Report dated March 15, 2009, by Gregory B. Saathoff M.D. Diplomate, American Board of Psychiatry and Neurology (FORENSIC PSYCHIATRIC EVALUATION)

Gregory B. Saathoff was asked by the United States Attorney's Office for the Southern District of New York to provide an independent psychiatric evaluation of Dr. Aafia to determine her current competency to stand trial. On February 12 and 13, he conducted a psychiatric evaluation of Dr. Aafia at the Federal Medical Center (FMC) Carswell in Fort Worth, Texas. The evaluation was attempted in three separate interview sessions and one-period of extended observation for a total of four hours. The timing and length of interview sessions were determined by Dr. Aafia's repeated refusal to be evaluated and requests for prayer-time as well as the FMC's visiting schedule for medical evaluation. Mr. Gregory's evaluation was based on examination interviews of Dr. Aafia, interviews of medical, nursing and security personnel at MDC Brooklyn, FMC Carswell, and review of documents.

He found Dr. Aafia's use of deception, evasiveness, expressions of paranoia and isolation as well as her public expression of psychotic symptoms and claim of torture, to have a significant impact on the assessment process. He saw her as showing dramatic yet inconsistently expressed hallucinations and delusions. Mr. Gregory further analyzed that Dr. Aafia's symptoms of mood disorder and cognitive dysfunction has complicated the picture for those who were responsible for evaluating her. He saw Dr. Aafia's high level of interpersonal and intellectual skills and ability to negotiate terms of her assessment have paradoxically served to impede assessment.

Mr. Gregory believed that symptoms Dr. Aafia had claimed in support of her refusal to continue with the legal process didn't bear up to close scrutiny for the following reasons:

1. Observable behavioral evidence of anxiety, mood, and cognitive disorders claimed by Dr. Aafia such as increased insomnia, decreased weight, amnesia, inability to read, inability to write and increased crying spells are contradicted by interviews of security and medical personnel at the MDC Brooklyn and the FMC Carswell, as well as objective monitoring documentation. A thorough review of the MDC Brooklyn log book for the two months she was detained there revealed that contrary to her claims, objective measures of her mental health such

as time spent eating, sleeping, praying, writing, reading, and attending to hygiene actually improved while the amount of time she was observed to be crying actually decreased.

2. Claimed psychotic symptoms that have included delusions and auditory and visual hallucinations have been inconsistent and have been accompanied by behaviors typically expected to accompany those symptoms. Review of documentation and interviews with staff contradicted her reports of psychotic behavior while at MDC Brooklyn and FMC Carswell. Review of the videotape of her physical examination at MDC Brooklyn reveals that at the time of the exam she was keenly aware of the purpose of the examination, the purpose of the cameras and the fact that members of the team were actually MDC Brooklyn personnel, not the dark angels that she later referenced. In fact, transcripts of her statements during the forced exams demonstrated that she repeatedly exhorted the staff to keep the cameras running for most of the exam so that others could later view treatment she felt was disrespectful to her.

3. Aafia had consistently refused to be assessed for purposes of the court. She had been selectively cooperative when attempts had been made to examine her through physical exams, psychiatric interviews and psychological testing. Her repeated refusals to comply with psychological testing, to cooperate with the psychiatric examiners sent by the government, and to answer most of their questions demonstrate an awareness that such cooperation could lead to an assessment of competency. Despite improvement that she attributed to her answered prayers made to Allah, she clearly indicated that she would continue to refuse to cooperate with any reassessment of competency and that the original determination of incompetency obtained in NOV 2008 should stand.

4. Psychotic symptoms of the magnitude claimed by Aafia were characteristic of individuals with major mental illnesses requiring psychotherapy and medication treatment. Remarkably, these dramatic hallucinations and delusions involving infants, dark angels, a dog in her cell and children visiting her in her room largely resolved after she was found to be incompetent to stand trial. Ultimately, these purported psychotic symptoms disappeared without the use of any psychotherapy or antipsychotic medication.

5. Dr. Aafia's comments to mental health professionals had suggested that she does not understand the basic elements of the judicial process. Aafia's comments to non-mental health professionals have revealed an understanding of the charges against her and the role of prosecution and defense attorneys as well as the role of prosecution expert witnesses who had been ordered by the court to perform an assessment.

Mr. Gregory in agreement with Dr. Aafia's treating psychiatrist and evaluating psychologist Dr. Kempke at FMC Carswell, concluded that Dr. Aafia does not have any major mental illness. Mr. Gregory evaluated that Dr. Aafia's constellations of varied, dramatic and evolving symptoms that she uses to "crowd the canvas" are much more consistent with malingered mental illness than true major mental illness. He said motivation to malinger generally involves either circumventing punishment or seeking pleasure. In Dr. Aafia's unique case, malingered symptoms had provided a dual solution in that a finding of incompetency could serve to both prevent prosecution while at the same time facilitating rapid repatriation to Pakistan. Therefore, in Mr. Gregory's opinion, Dr. Aafia had sufficient present ability to consult with her lawyers with a reasonable degree of rational understanding and maintained a rational as well as factual understanding of the proceedings against her. Therefore, Dr. Aafia was competent to stand trial[218].

Detailed Report dated March 16, 2009, by Sally C. Johnson M.D. Professor, Department of Psychiatry. The University of North Carolina at Chapel Hill (Johnson Report)

For purpose of evaluation Ms. Johnson had received and reviewed extensive collateral information such as audio files, videotapes, copies of some documents retrieved from the thumb drive found in Dr. Aafia's possession, notes by other government psychiatrist Mr. Gregory of 01/13/09, interviews of certain MDC Brooklyn staff who observed inmate Dr. Aafia and made inmate entries to the logbook, copies of additional medical records and progress notes obtained from FMC Carswell. Ms. Johnson also reviewed a copy of Dr. Aafia dissertation's *"Separating the components of Imitation,"* copy of Dr. Aafia's academic transcripts from MIT and Brandeis University. She questioned a list of individuals in contact with Dr. Aafia while in transport to the United States, and additional material provided by FMC Carswell and MDC Brooklyn, such as medical files, psychological files, central files, and an article co-authored by Dr. Aafia entitled "Reproduction of Scene Actions: Stimulus Selective Learning", which was published in *Perception* 2003, Volume 32, pages 138-854. Ms. Johnson was initially asked by defense counsel Fink to speak with defense retained experts, but no one contacted Ms. Johnson. She did talk to Dr. Aafia's new court-appointed attorney Ms. Dawn Cardi and Chud Edgar.

Ms. Johnson observed Dr. Aafia's behavior while interviewing her and made an extensive report. The major extract of the report in her own words is as follows:

Initially, Dr. Aafia was extremely uncooperative with the evaluation process during my visits to the FMC, Carswell. Her behavior within the interview setting was inconsistent with the behavior and verbalizations noted when she was unaware that she was under direct observation. Initially, she was approached by the nursing staff to request that she come to the conference room to begin the evaluation, but she refused to leave her room. Then I subsequently went to her room with the nurse manager so she could introduce me as an evaluator and explain the evaluation process. Dr. Aafia clearly stated that she did not want to be involved in the evaluation and she will not cooperate with the evaluation process. She indicated that she had already completed an evaluation in regard to her competency to stand trial and she had no intent of complying with any further evaluation. It was again explained to Dr. Aafia who am I and what the purpose of the evaluation process was. She then stated that the judge has already told her that she was dead and that she could not cooperate with the evaluation process because it would result in her daughter being raped and killed. When an effort was made to continue talking with her, she tried to leave the room and then sat on the floor indicating she would refuse to cooperate. She was encouraged to come to the conference room but refused to do so. She asked that the nurse supervisor remain in the doorway as long as I was there. She then bent over covering her face and attempted to appear as if she was sobbing, stating over and over again that her daughter would be raped and killed. This behavior was observed for some length, and an effort was made to reassure her, and she was asked to share more about her concerns for her daughter. She indicated that she was not going to listen to anything I had to say and that she was going to put her fingers in her ears so that she could not hear. She proceeded to do so and continued sitting on the floor.

What followed was an extended period of observation during which her symptoms presentation did not appear consistent with any identifiable psychiatric diagnosis. She attempted to appear to be crying, but no tears were evident. There was no evidence of any anxiety. Although she insisted she could not hear, she intermittently commented on something being said by the nursing staff to me. She periodically switched fingers, leaving one ear uncovered, thus it was obvious she was listening to the conversations. After a while, she began talking about her children coming to visit her in the unit and persistently attempted to seek validation from the nursing staff in regard to this. When the nurse manager indicated that it was not permitted to have children or anyone visit in the unit and that all visitations had to occur in the visiting room, Dr. Aafia made comments such as "You are not going to stop them from coming, are you? I told them to be very quiet, and I have talked to all of the other inmates on the unit, they don't mind if they come." When the nurse manager didn't engage in discussion on that topic, Dr. Aafia attempted to provide additional details about this possible hallucinatory experience. When asked specific questions as to the size of her children and the clothing they were wearing, she described them as very small and described that her son was wearing a jumper or gym suit. When the nurse manager commented that the children might be small because Dr. Aafia was a small woman, she emphasized that was not the case, and reiterated that her son was very small. She appeared much invested in getting the nurse manager to sympathize with her situation and believe her story.

Dr. Aafia adamantly refused to answer any specific questions in regard to her history or her understanding of her legal situation, her relation with her attorney, or her familiarity with the legal process. Periodically, Dr. Aafia would interject that she didn't intend to be disrespectful, but that she could not cooperate because of what would happen to her daughter.

After approximately two hours during which it was evident that Dr. Aafia was tired of sitting on the floor and keeping her fingers in her ears, I told her that they would stop for the moment, but would resume as the day progressed. Later in the afternoon, two additional attempts were made to interview Dr. Aafia. Initially, when given the option to continue the eval-uation that afternoon or the following morning, she elected to continue in the afternoon. Shortly thereafter, however, she continued with the behav-ior of stating that she was not going to listen to anything I said or asked and that she was not going to cooperate. She made the statement that she would continue to put her fingers in her ears and not listen to me until her ears turned red.

On the third attempt to interview her, her roommate was in her room. When I pointed out that it was unfair of her to monopolize the room to continue the evaluation and it would be preferable to continue in the conference room, Dr. Aafia stopped her complaint regarding her fear that her daughter would be raped and killed. She calmly turned to her roommate and asked if she would mind finding another place to be for a period of time, such as the TV room. When her roommate didn't immediately respond, she verbalized to her roommate that she had never asked any favor of her before so she was hopeful that she would cooperate and give her some privacy. Her roommate did cooperate and left the room. Once her roommate left, Dr. Aafia again indicated that she had no intention of cooperating with the evaluation and that she was not going to provide any history or answer any questions asked by me. She indicated that she wanted the nursing staff to be present and would not go to the conference room. I pulled up a chair at the door of her room to attempt to continue the evaluation, but Dr. Aafia continued to refuse to cooperate. The interview was eventually terminated with Dr. Aafia being told it would continue the following morning.

During the second day of the interview process, Dr. Aafia was noted to be eating in her room and was smiling and laughing with the unit officer, until such time when she was directly approached by me for the continuation of the interview. At that point she indicated that she was not going to be part of the evaluation, stating that she was used to torture sessions and was not going to cooperate. She again put her fingers in her ears, stating "I can't hear you, I am not listening." She closed her eyes and sat down in her chair. I again reviewed the reasons for the evaluation and the limits of confidentiality. She continued to keep her eyes closed, plugged her ears and refused to cooperate. At that point, the nurse manager again came by. Dr. Aafia asked the nurse if she had to stay to talk with me. Dr. Aafia was told that I would not continue the evaluation in her room and she would need to move to an office or conference room. With insistence she did come into the nurse manager office where again an attempt was made to review her history, to assess her understanding of the legal proceedings and her readiness to work with her attorneys in her own defense. She adamantly refused to answer any questions in regard to these issues and refused to provide information even on very simple questions such as her age or the date. At one point the nurse manager who had remained in the area took a break to go the restroom. Dr. Aafia stated that she would not stay in the room with me and stood out in the hall until the nurse manager returned. While in the hall she was observed to be engaged in conversation with individuals not involved in the evaluation process without any apparent distress. Continued efforts throughout the day to engage her in cooperating with the evaluation brought about similar behavior, again not consistent with any specific psychiatric diagnoses.

Indirectly, it was clear that Dr. Aafia was orientated to person, time, place and situation, although she refused to directly answer questions in regard to her orientation. She appeared aware of the time of the day, was able to assemble for mealtime appropriately and responded appropriately to counts. It was clear that from one day to the next and from one evaluation period to the next, she retained memory of the purpose of the evaluation and of the identity of the evaluator. She was also able to accurately reference various questions or issues that were raised during the evaluation process to other staff and in phone conversations. She refused to cooperate with any formal assessment of her memory. It was clear that Dr. Aafia had processed the rules and regulations at the institution. Despite her aggravation with the evaluation process, she maintained impulse control. She appeared to have made the decision that it would be in her best interest not to cooperate with the evaluation. She appeared to be aware that she had previously been found not competent to stand trial by Dr. Powers. As noted, she was not viewed as a reliable reporter of psychiatric symptomatology.

Once Ms. Johnson finished interviewing Dr. Aafia and reviewed all the information, she made the following conclusions:

1. Dr. Aafia had expressed awareness to various individuals of the charges against her. She had also described alternative

accounts of the events to various individuals. There is no indication that she had any delusional ideas about her actions at the time of the events.

2. Dr. Aafia did not demonstrate any clear problem with memory. Her ability to respond to simple questions regarding her age, birthplace, were not consistent with someone actually suffering a memory impairment, but more an issue of her willingness to provide information. Within the interview sessions, during observed conversations, and through review of collateral, it was clear that her short term, intermediate and long term memory was intact. There was no indication that she could not remember or process information that was provided to her and retained it for a sufficient period of time to assist her attorneys and complete legal proceedings should she chose to do so.

3. Dr. Aafia had made several attempts to bargain with information in regard to her current situation. It appeared that she had the capacity to understand the plea bargaining process should she chose to do so.

4. Dr. Aafia was aware that she had been charged with serious crimes, was facing prosecution, and had knowledge of the specific charges and potential penalties if convicted. She understood that the prosecution's account of what occurred was different than the account which she would like to put forth.

5. Dr. Aafia had demonstrated an ability to behave appropriately on the Housing Unit. At times, she had demonstrated histrionic behavior and expressed anger when she did not agree with tasks at hand. Nonetheless, even when expressing that she was stressed and upset with this evaluator's attempts to accomplish her interests. It appeared that she could control her behavior in a courtroom should she chose to do so.

6. Dr. Aafia's attorneys described limited interactions with her and briefly described a breakdown in their communication with her. They suggested this was related to her reaction to the strip search process. However, it was clear that the strip search process itself had not interfered with her continuing to visit others as demonstrated by her meeting in the visiting room with her brother many times, and it had not precluded her from choosing to meet with the Pakistani consulate members. This supported that she was not so traumatized by the process that she was unable to meet with her attorneys within the structure of her current custody in the Federal Bureau of Prisons. Again, her willingness to meet with her attorneys seemed to be a choice on her part rather than a product of any mental disease or defect.

7. Dr. Aafia was not suffering from any type of anxiety or impulse control disorder which would interfere with her ability to attend to proceedings during the trial. She appeared to have sufficient impulse control to maintain proper courtroom decorum.

8. An effort was made throughout this evaluation period to offer general information to Dr. Aafia about the courtroom process, principle courtroom personnel, available pleas, possible defenses, the plea bargaining process and the appeals process.

9. Dr. Aafia appeared to understand that legal representation was designed to assist her in fairly moving through the legal process.

10. Dr. Aafia appeared to be interested in retaining an attorney to assist her in her situation; she simply didn't wish to work with initial attorneys who had been assigned to her. At the same time, early in the process, she did verbalize an awareness that if viewed as competent she could ask to change her attorneys

and also appeared to understand that she could privately retain attorneys should she be able to do so financially. There was evidence in her conversations with her brother that she was motivated to have him continue to explore alternate legal representation and to raise funds for her legal defense.

In Ms. Johnson's opinion Dr. Aafia was not presently suffering from a mental disease or defect rendering her mentally incompetent to the extent she was unable to understand the nature and consequences of the proceedings or assist properly with her defense. She said Dr. Aafia had a rational and factual understanding of the proceedings against her and was able to assist her attorneys with a reasonable degree of rational understanding should she chose to do so.[219]

Detailed Report dated May 4, 2009, by Leslie Powers Ph.D.

The initial Forensic evaluation report dated November 6, 2008, was opinioned by Forensic Psychologist Leslie Powers Ph.D. In this report, Ms. Powers interviewed Dr. Aafia and declared her incompetent to stand trial as a result of her mental illness. On May 4, 2009 report, Dr. Powers interviewed Dr. Aafia again and made the following observations:

"In the absence of any collateral documents concerning Dr. Aafia's mental health history, the diagnosis of Major Depressive Disorder in the November 2008 report was based on her Depressive symptomatology, her disinterest in participating in activities, and her self-report of appetite, sleep, and concentration difficulties. After nearly six months of observation and review of the extensive collateral evidence that has since been made available to her, she now believed that Dr. Aafia's response when she first arrived was due, in part, to a reaction to facing criminal prosecution and incarceration. Initially, Dr. Aafia showed little, if any psychological distress for the first two months in US custody, despite having been monitored on a continual basis at both Bagram Air Force Base and MDC Brooklyn and interviewed extensively for hours at a time by an FBI investigator. When she did report experiencing sadness and tearfulness,

Dr. Aafia stated it was 'related to the gravity of her legal difficulties.' Over time, she has been noted to be tearful and to present with dysthymic affect in situationally appropriate times, but not outside the realm of a normal adjustment to a new situation."

Dr. Powers further added that in the November 2008 report, a diagnosis of Posttraumatic Stress Disorder (PTSD) was offered but was ruled out as more information became available and Dr. Aafia was monitored over time. She said no evidence of political torture had been presented for this evaluation that would be an antecedent for this disorder. She said Dr. Aafia had consistently been a poor historian, as she had steadfastly refused to provide any information that would clarify any questions regarding her exposure to trauma. She said Dr. Aafia did not exhibit the psychological symptoms that would warrant a diagnosis of Posttraumatic Stress Disorder.

Dr. Powers concluded that Dr. Aafia meets the diagnostic criteria for Malingering. Therefore, in Dr. Powers' professional opinion, Dr. Aafia was currently competent to stand trial. She further said Dr. Aafia was not suffering from a mental disease or defect which would render her unable to understand the nature and consequences of the proceedings against her or to assist properly in her own defense.[220]

Detailed Report dated June 20, 2009, by L. Thomas Kucharski Ph.D. Chair Department of Psychology John Jay College of Criminal Justice (Kucharski Report)

The Defense retained Mental Health Professional Mr. Thomas Kucharski submitted his Forensic Psychological Evaluation report to the court on June 20, 2009.

For the purpose of evaluation, Ms. Kucharski had reviewed extensive information such as documents, audio files, videotapes, the Forensic Psychiatric Evaluation Report of Gregory B. Saathoff MD dated 03/15/09, and conducted collateral interviews with Dr. Aafia's brother Mohammed Siddiqui, her sister Fowzia Siddiqui, and mental health staff at FMC Carswell. Nursing staff and the officer who was admitted at the Facility were briefly interviewed. Attempts were made to interview the mental health staff at MDC Brooklyn but weren't allowed. Ms. Dawn Cardi and Chad Edgar were consulted throughout the evaluation process. Asif Hussain, a representative of the Pakistani embassy who met with Dr. Siddiqui on a number of occasions, was interviewed on June 16, 2009.

Mr. Thomas observed Dr. Aafia's behavior while interviewing her and made an extensive report. The major extract of the report in her own words is as follows:

Dr. Aafia was interviewed in her room at the FMC Carswell. She was extremely guarded, willing to provide only limited information, and often refused to answer certain questions. She attempted to control the interview, spoke to the nurse who was present, and had little eye contact with me. Dr. Aafia's eye contact improved as the interview proceeded. Dr. Aafia's thinking was very tangential moving from topic to topic in a disconnected manner. Her thoughts were replete with numerous conspiratorial ideas, some of which are consistent with radical political beliefs others not. For example, she spoke at length about conspiracies by the Jews, Israel, India, and the United States. She spoke to agents about India building dams that resulted in many Pakistanis dying of thirst. She also related a number of beliefs that appeared delusional. For example, she believed that she was being poisoned and that staff at the facility were intending to kill her. She related that it was known to the inmates that a specific unnamed staff member took psychotropic medications. She stated that he, therefore, could kill her in her sleep and would not be punished because he would get off on an insanity defense. Furthermore, she reported she believed that during the forced medical evaluation where blood was taken, she was also injected with an unknown substance. She spoke at length about being dead; having been killed during the strip searches performed at MDC Brooklyn. This report of being dead had a metaphorical quality as she also appeared to be aware that she was alive as she made many statements about not caring what happened to her in the future. She reported the naked video of her during the strip search was put on the internet for everyone to view. This humiliation, the belief that she will never leave prison or see her children, that she has been shamed and thus would be an outcast in the Muslim world and her community appears to be what she is referring to as being dead. She believes the court is responsible for this humiliation and has "already killed her." She believes that she was responsible for the fate of other inmates in the unit in that her engagement with them resulted in them receiving disciplinary actions.[221]

Mr. Thomas also gave observations on Dr. Aafia's Mental Status as follow:

Throughout the records, Dr. Aafia has denied being mentally ill and as having very poor insight into her mental illness. From time to time she questions whether she is "going crazy," but this is related to the stress she is experiencing and not an acceptance of her current psychiatric difficulties. She admitted to brief fleeting visions of her children, of a man standing outside her cell and of a dog eating off a plate. These visions appear to be hypnagogic experiences and not true visual hallucinations. They are not enduring experiences that typically characterize true visual hallucinations. There appears to be no auditory, tactile or olfactory hallucinations. Significant depression has been noted throughout her incarceration. The outward effective presentation of depression has vacillated and at the same time of this interview may have diminished to some degree as she was able to smile, her energy level appeared adequate, and she engaged in the discussion with some vigor. However, there was profound hopelessness, helplessness and sadness particularly centered on the wellbeing of her children. She has repeatedly denied suicidal ideation stating that her fate is in God's hand.

Sleep and appetite appears to be significantly disturbed. Dr. Aafia complains about concentration difficulties that limit her ability to read the Quran, although she spends significant energy trying to read the Quran. Social Interaction is significantly limited. She spends much of her time isolated in her room. Dr. Aafia appears oriented to person, place and time although her understanding of her current circumstances appears to involve some delusional interpretation. Judgment appears limited particularly around her legal representation and cooperation. There were no significant intellectual deficits, no severe memory impairment, although some concentration and therefore short term memory deficits of minor proportion are likely. No abnormal movements were noted. Her speech was tangential but of normal rate. Records of her interviews with the FBI were suggestive of some grandiose thinking as are some of her writings. No symptoms of mania were observed. Her demeanor was quite paranoid. It is noteworthy that the interview with her brother revealed phenomena very characteristic of those with paranoid delusional disorder.[222]

After review of the medical records, the transcripts of telephone conversations, collateral interviews with mental health staff, 302 investigative reports of the FBI, the forensic evaluations submitted by Doctors including Johnson, Saathoff, and Powers, Dr. Aafia's writings and materials found on her following her arrest, it was Mr. Thomas' opinion that Dr. Aafia was suffering from mental illness best characterized as a Delusional Disorder of the Paranoid Type. He further said that Dr. Aafia was also significantly depressed with symptoms of hopelessness, helplessness, sleep difficulties, and poor concentrations.

It was also Mr. Thomas' opinion there was very strong evidence Dr. Aafia was not malingering. Mr. Thomas' opinion was based on the following:

1. First and most important, Dr. Aafia denies being mentally ill. I have studied many ways to detect malingering and denial of psychiatric disorder. It is virtually unheard of that a defendant attempting to portray herself as mentally ill and malinger psychiatric disorder would go to such efforts to deny mental illness. Malingerers go to great length to convince evaluators that they suffer from extreme psychiatric symptoms. In spite

of repeated reference to the denial of psychiatric disorder cited by Dr. Johnson, she opines that Dr. Aafia is malingering.

2. Dr. Aafia has avoided mental health professionals, and on one occasion going so far as to retreat her request to see psychology services at MDC Brooklyn for fear that they would "think she is crazy." Being viewed as crazy is exactly what the malingerers seek. Malingerers go out of their way to draw attention to their feigned mental illness. Dr. Aafia does exactly the opposite, avoids mental health professionals and tries to conceal her psychiatric difficulties. On the trip to New York from Afghanistan, she related a number of beliefs, mostly conspiratorial to FBI agents. On arrival at MDC Brooklyn, she denied all symptoms. Her intake screening was devoid of any psychiatric concerns. As opposed to trying to impress the mental health staff of her symptoms she concealed them. Mental health staff at MDC Brooklyn utilized an approach where they stayed out of view of Dr. Aafia while she conversed with correctional staff as a means of overcoming her unwillingness to discuss her symptoms with mental health staff openly. She has consistently refused mental health treatment or services.

3. Dr. Aafia presents with symptoms that are difficult to feign. Specifically, she has uniformly been viewed by mental health staff and layperson as tangential, irrelevant, with a flight of ideas. Maintaining a consistent thought pattern and speech that rambles to irrelevancies requires a high level of concentration, focus, and persistence that is rarely possible. She evidenced significant sleep disorder at MDC Brooklyn with a documented record of one or two hours sleep over a significant period.

4. There is behavioral confirmation of her hypnagogic experiences. Note that the logbook entry of the officer observing her noted she was behaving strangely at 2:20 am on the morning she reported seeing the dog in her cell.

5. She has been extraordinarily consistent in her symptom presentation to the mental health staff, her brother and Mr. Hussain. All shared she reported being dead as well as her hypnagogic experiences and her conspiratorial ideas regarding Jews, India and the United States. All reported being informed about attempts to murder, poison, or otherwise harm her. Malingerers have difficulty maintaining such consistency across different contexts. They usually don't see the need to convince other than the mental health staff of their feigned symptoms.

6. Most malingerers attempt to convince evaluators that they experience ongoing auditory hallucinations, that are persistent, continuous, uncontrollable and that they are unable to adapt to the hallucinations. Malingerers are required to simply report that they are hearing voices, a presentation that requires little effort. Dr. Aafia has reported fleeting visuals hypnogogic experiences common to those with depression and those who are sleep deprived. They are thematically related to her lost children and very connected to the worries and fears she has for their wellbeing. They are not persistent, persuasive, nor do they dramatically impact her everyday behavior. This is in contrast to Dr. Saathoff's claim that their diminishing over time is evidence of malingering. This might represent the normal course of these experiences as she adjusts to her situation.

7. If Dr. Aafia is malingering, she would be capable of fully understanding the consequences of being found mentally ill and incompetent. This would include the likelihood of

involuntary treatment with antipsychotic medication, something she will find very difficult to accept. If not restored she will become subject to dangerousness proceedings pursuant to section 4246 and civil commitment potentially for the rest of her life. Therefore, there is very little secondary gain to being found incompetent. Clearly, Dr. Aafia is very intelligent and if not mentally ill would be very careful of assessing these risks. In her case, in reality, there is no secondary gain and potentially a greater risk.

8. Dr. Aafia is very guarded and refuses to speak in any detail about the domestic violence and any past trauma. Malingerers are overly forthcoming when discussing past trauma as they believe that trauma and abuse are etiologically significant. Those who are abused find it very difficult to speak about past trauma while malingerers are overly willing to address past trauma often bringing up traumatic experience without even being asked. Such a presentation is characteristic of malingering.[223]

COMPETENCY HEARING

On July 6, 2009, the court had a competency hearing. Dr. Aafia was present in the court with attorney Dawn Cardi. The Forensic Evaluation reports by all psychiatrists, Sally C. Johnson M.D., Gregory B. Saathoff, M.D. and L. Thomas Kucharski, Ph.D. were submitted in the court in lieu of direct testimony.

The hearing included the cross-examination and redirect examination of all three psychiatrists. With the consent of the government and defense attorneys the court also received into evidence the deposition testimony of Leslie Powers, PhD., dated June 26, 2009, and deposition testimony of Camille Kempke, M.D., dated July 01, 2009, and numerous exhibits (agreed to by Attorney).

In summary, the Government argued that the testimony and other evidence presented in this hearing establishes that Dr. Aafia is malingering and doesn't suffer from a mental disease or defect. In addition, the evidence establishes that Dr. Aafia possesses a rational and factual understanding of the proceedings, and possesses the ability to consult with her attorney with a reasonable degree of rational understanding.

In summary, the defense argued that Dr. Aafia was not presently competent to stand trial because of her delusional disorder and her tangential thinking. Both her delusional disorder and tangential thinking rendered Dr. Aafia unable to understand the proceedings against her and prevented her from providing assistance to her attorneys. As a criminal attorney's most fundamental tasks were to obtain from their client a clear account of the events surrounding the alleged offense conducted and to subject that account to inevitable questions and inevitably, challenges, the fact Dr. Aafia's mental state precludes both of these fundamental tasks meant she could not lend assistance to her attorneys.

During the hearing, the court observed the demeanor and assessed the credibility of each of the witnesses. The court also observed the demeanor of Dr. Aafia in the courtroom. The court found that Dr. Dr. Aafia is competent to stand trial by the preponderance of the evidence. The court also found that Dr. Aafia had sufficient present ability to consult with her lawyers with a reasonable degree of rational understanding and she also had a rational as well as a factual understanding of the proceeding against her, hence satisfying the Dusky test.[224]

Chapter 7

Dr. Aafia And
The Defence Attorneys

*T*HROUGHOUT THE TRIAL HEARINGS, DR.
Aafia had disagreements and dissatisfaction with her attorneys. In this chapter, I have mentioned in detail all such events from the court documents and transcripts that will help one to analyze whether there was (any) complete breakdown of communication between Dr. Aafia and her attorneys during the trial hearings.

On August 5, 2008, Dr. Aafia appeared before the Magistrate court judge Ronald L. Ellis in the Southern District Court of New York. Judge R.L. Ellis told Dr. Aafia that she had the right to be represented by counsel during all court proceedings and during all questioning by the authorities. Dr. Aafia completed a financial affidavit indicating she had no assets, property and is neither employed nor any income. Elizabeth Fink who was the CJA attorney on duty that day in the Magistrate court was appointed by the Judge to represent Dr. Aafia. Fink then introduced Elaine Whitfield Sharp (Attorney in the District of Massachusetts) to the court, who was not retained by Dr. Aafia but by the family of Dr. Aafia for the purpose of the proceedings.[225] On August 11, 2008, Fink requested Magistrate court judge Henry B. Pitman to admit Elaine Whitfield Sharp as pro hac vice for the purpose of the case.[226]

On September 4, 2008, Fink introduced her two young associates Sarah Kunstler and Gideon Oliver to District Court Judge Richard Berman. In addition, she also introduced Elaine Sharp, who had been admitted by Judge Pitman as pro hac vice to represent Dr. Aafia's family in the court. Judge Berman asked Elaine Sharp if she was representing Dr. Aafia's family's interest in the case. Elaine Sharp replied with a "yes" and said that Dr. Aafia had asked her to represent her in the case, too. Judge Berman replied that Dr. Aafia was entitled to choose whomever she wishes as her counsel either Sharp or Fink, but the court needed to discuss this issue further in the near future. Judge Berman notified Elaine Sharp that since she was not the counsel on record, therefore any document under discussion in court will not be available to her unless it hits the public docket or she could request Fink for the curtsey copy of the document.[227]

On September 23, 2008, during the status conference, Fink apprised the court that Dr. Aafia was in mental pain, was unable to make a mental determination and needed to be treated in a hospital setting. Fink further added Dr. Aafia had refused to communicate with her counsel or to open her legal mail; therefore she was not competent to stand trial.[228] On the other hand, the Government requested the court to order a complete psychiatric exam along with a report prepared by the psychiatrist and order a competency hearing before the court to determine Dr. Aafia's competency to stand trial.[229]

In response to the court order dated October 1, 2008, the court received a psychological evaluation report, dated November 6, 2008, by Leslie Powers, Ph.D., forensic psychologist, United States Department of Justice, Federal Bureau of Prisons, Federal Medical Center, Carswell. The report concluded that Dr. Aafia was incompetent to stand trial as a result of her mental illness. Dr. Powers diagnosed Dr. Aafia with Major Depressive Disorder Severe with Mood Congruent Psychotic Features based on her depressive symptomology, her disinterest in participating in activities, and her self-report of appetite, sleep and concentration difficulties.[230]

Thereafter, both government and defense counsel retained their own respective mental health professionals to conduct additional psychiatric analysis and evaluation of Dr. Aafia. During the evaluation, the psychiatrists conducted many interviews with several individuals, including Dr. Aafia's attorneys and the staff who observed Dr. Aafia during her stay at MDC Brooklyn and Carswell. The psychiatrists also reviewed draft transcripts of telephone conversations between Dr. Aafia and her brother Mohammed Siddiqui and Pakistan Consulate Official Mr. Asif Hussain.

A draft transcript of Dr. Aafia's telephone conversation with her brother on August 29, 2008, revealed that Dr. Aafia advised her brother to get help from the President of Pakistan Legal Forum, Texas, in hiring an attorney for her case. She also advised her brother to raise funds for hiring the attorney.[231] Dr. Aafia's attorneys during an interview with the evaluator described limited interaction with Dr. Aafia and described a brief breakdown in communication with her.[232]

On February 23, 2009, during the conference hearing, Fink made an application to the court to be relieved from the case for personal reasons, particularly medical reasons. The court granted her application and appointed CJA attorney Dawn Cardi to succeed Elizabeth Fink.[233]

On July 6, 2009, the court held a competency hearing. Dr. Aafia was present in the court with attorney Dawn Cardi. The Forensic Evaluation reports by both Government and Defense psychiatrists were submitted in the court. The Government argued, "that the testimony and other evidence presented in this hearing establishes that the defendant is malingering and doesn't suffer from a mental disease or defect." The defense argued that Dr. Aafia was not presently competent to stand trial because of her delusional disorder and her tangential thinking. The court found that Dr. Aafia had sufficient present ability to consult with her attorneys with a reasonable degree of rational understanding and she also had a rational as well as a factual understanding of the proceeding against her, hence satisfying the standard set forth in the *United States v Dusky 362 U.S.402 (1960)*. The court also concluded that Dr. Aafia understood the nature of the charges against her and could assist counsel in her defense and hence was competent to stand trial.[234]

By letter dated August 11, 2009, attorney Charles Swift apprised the court that following this court determination Dr. Aafia was competent to stand trial, the Government of Pakistan elected to exercise its right under *Section (c) of Article 36 of the Vienna Convention for Consular Relations*, to retain counsels on Dr. Aafia's behalf. He said that this determination was made in consultation with Dr. Aafia's family and with the understanding she adamantly refused to be represented by her Court Appointed Counsel Dawn Cardi. Charles Swift also said that on August 10, 2009, Pakistan entered into agreements with him, Linda Moreno and Elaine Sharp to represent Dr. Aafia, with the understanding that Ms. Moreno would act as the lead counsel while Dawn Cardi and Ms. Sharp would be the associate counsel. He said in each of the agreements the attorneys made clear their duty of loyalty lay with Dr. Aafia and that they would zealously represent her regardless of Pakistan's interest.

Charles Swift also wrote in a letter that Ms. Sharp spoke with Dr. Aafia on the telephone. During this phone conversation, Ms. Sharp disclosed that Pakistan had provided funds for a defense team to represent Dr. Aafia and sought her permission to enter into the case on her behalf. She said Dr. Aafia initially focused on and reaffirmed she didn't want to be represented by appointed counsel. When questioned regarding her willingness to be represented by counsel retained by Pakistan on her behalf, Dr. Aafia didn't expressly oppose the representation. However, she didn't affirmatively assent to it either. Unable to secure a decision, Ms. Sharp ended the phone call.

He also wrote that he himself and Ms. Moreno had filed Notice of Appearance in the case and Motions for Admission pro hac vice without delay, and Ms. Sharp likewise intended to file such notice and motion as soon as practicable. He said Ms. Moreno also proposed the court the following course of action:

1. That Ms. Dawn Cardi remain on the case and not to be released by the court until such time that Aafia affirmatively elects representation by undersigned counsel

2. That myself, Moreno and Swift be authorized access to all the discovery

3. That upon transmission of proof of required security clearance to the court Security officer, Ms. Moreno and myself be permitted the access to classified discovery, if such discovery is or has been provided, and

4. That in keeping with the court motion calendar, all counsels file motions jointly unless counsel's ethical or professional obligations require separate fillings[235]

By the letter dated August 14, 2009, the prosecution attorney respectfully proposed to the court that a conference hearing be held, during which the court would question the defendant regarding how she wanted to proceed with respect to her representation. The letter also stated that the government believed that CJA attorney should remain the sole counsel of record, unless and until Dr. Aafia affirmatively consents to have another attorney to represent her. The letter further added the government did not believe that the defendant should, without further inquiry, be represented both by CJA counsel and Proposed attorney. Therefore, the government requested the court schedule a conference to conduct an inquiry of the defendant, regarding the decision of whether she should be represented by CJA Counsel or Proposed Counsel.[236]

In response to the prosecution attorney's letter dated August 14, 2009, Dawn Cardi wrote to the court on August 17, 2009, that government proposal blissfully ignored the backdrop of mental health issues associated with Dr. Aafia, especially her delusional disorder which is particularly focused on the court system and any attorneys associated with it. She said, this court had declared Dr. Aafia competent to stand trial but had nevertheless recognized that Dr. Aafia had "some mental issue." Cardi also wrote that if the court believed, like she did, that Dr. Aafia was suffering from serious mental health issues, then the government request that Dr. Aafia comes to the court and simply state her "wishes" with respect to who she wishes to be represented was ill-advised at best.

She further wrote that after having represented Dr. Aafia for past six months, she believed that Dr. Aafia could not make a decision in her own self-interest, and in the spirit of governing ethical rules that addressed attorney conduct, where a client was suffering from diminished mental capacity, Cardi believe she was required to take protective action on Dr. Aafia's behalf. Therefore, she respectfully requests the court on her behalf that the attorneys (Linda Moreno, Charles Swift, and Elaine Sharp) Pakistan government had retained for Dr. Aafia be made co-counsel of record.

Dawn Cardi also wrote one US Supreme Court case reference cited *Indiana v Edwards, 128 S.Ct. 2388 (2008),* in which Supreme court held that the court could and should place limits on the legal decisions made by a mentally ill defendant found to be competent under *Dusky test* because the standard for competency to stand trial by no mean precluded the possibility a defendant like Dr. Aafia nonetheless suffered "from severe mental disorder."[237]

A conference hearing was held on September 2, 2009, in which Judge Berman placed the issue of Dr. Aafia's right to counsel and representation for discussion. Dr. Aafia and both prosecution and Defense counsel were present. Judge Berman confirmed that CJA attorney Elizabeth Fink was appointed for Dr. Aafia because she was unable to afford an attorney on her own. He said that Ms. Dawn Cardi had replaced Ms. Fink as her continued representation was not viable. In addition, the Government of Pakistan had retained three esteemed professionals (Mr.

Swift, Mr. Moreno and Ms. Sharp) as defense counsel to represent Dr. Aafia under Article 38 of the Vienna convention. Judge Berman remarked that it was somehow an unusual situation but, CJA attorney and the third party retained attorneys could work together as a team while Ms. Dawn Cardi could be a lead attorney in a sense to coordinate with the court. Ms. Dawn Cardi confirmed to the court it was a very viable way to proceed and would provide Dr. Aafia with the strongest defense. Dr. Aafia interjected and said she didn't agree with the team the court was putting together for her and the Pakistani Consulate had no right to do that. She said she had never given this right to anyone to form a team for her and she had already requested Ms. Dawn Cardi to stop representing her in court. Judge Berman said to Ms. Dawn Cardi that this would leave defense in an untenable position and Dr. Aafia's own interest would not be well served, however, she was welcome to any other counsels she wanted to retain. Dr. Aafia again said that she could not retain counsels of her own choice because she had been put in such conditions, but she didn't agree with the team provided to represent her. She said they couldn't impose people on someone without consent and she had other issues which she wanted to discuss and resolve peacefully. She confronted Judge Berman that he never gave her a chance to speak. Judge Berman said that it was in Dr. Aafia's best interest to speak through her attorneys but if she didn't then that was ultimately her prerogative and the attorneys were very proficient in their business. Mr. LaVigne, the prosecution attorney, added it was a very complicated and unusual situation and Dr. Aafia's Sixth Amendment right allowed her the right to counsel. He further said he believes the court should inquire Dr. Aafia about her objections regarding the attorneys.

Judge Berman said that Dr. Aafia doesn't want any of the attorneys there to represent her and if she was left without counsel then that would be a big mistake. He said he's safeguarding the interest of both parties. Dr. Aafia said that although she didn't agree with her lawyers, they are talking on her behalf without her consent and it also looks like Judge Berman was fighting this case for her. Mr. LaVigne said Dr. Aafia needs to be informed she has three choices; she could either choose Ms. Dawn Cardi alone, or the three attorneys who had been retained by the government of Pakistan alone or with Ms. Dawn Cardi or finally to represent herself. He said he understood it was difficult and there was also the possibility of Curcio hearing to investigate whether there's was a conflict of interest existing between attorneys retained by the government of Pakistan and Dr. Aafia's interest. He also said if there was a reason why Dr. Aafia didn't want these three attorneys on her case, then the court needs to explore the said reason. Judge Berman shared that Dr. Aafia has shown resistance to all attorneys even when Ms. Fink was her CJA counsel and if she has an alternative, she has never proposed any. Dr. Aafia abruptly said, "how about letting her find an attorney?" Judge Berman said it was too complicated. He said she has a very strong defense team and it didn't get any stronger. Dr. Aafia again said she didn't agree with her attorneys. Judge Berman again asked if she had any alternative. Dr. Aafia replied that how she could have any when she was locked up and was not able to make a phone call or talk. She said she had not hired anyone for the case because nobody was willing to talk on her behalf. Ms. Dawn Cardi said that part of the reason she didn't participate in the meetings with her attorneys was because she has to be strip searched in order to meet them. Ms. Sharp said she would be pleased to work with the government and they could come to some agreement regarding the strip searching to enhance the possibility of them meeting Dr. Aafia. The court confirmed the date of September 23, 2009, for the hearing to address strip search issue.[238]

During the September 23, 2009, conference hearing the court notified the defense attorneys of a positive development on the strip search issue. Judge Berman said that Dr. Aafia didn't have to undergo strip searches before meeting her counsel at MDC. He thanked government and defense attorneys and bureau of prisons for their co-operation on this issue. Ms. Sharp added that due to that development, the defense attorneys had full seven-hour meetings with Dr. Aafia in the last seven days alone, and they are very happy with it. Judge Berman said there was no need for

Curcio hearing, as he had determined there was no potential conflict of interest existing in attorneys retained by the government of Pakistan for Dr. Aafia's interest. He said, Dr. Aafia had never indicated she wanted to exercise the right of self-determination, and Dr. Aafia had expressed no realistic or viable plan to have a change of attorney. He further said that in his estimation, Ms. Dawn Cardi and the three newest attorneys had well represented her so far and he had no basis or reason to doubt the competent representation and that it would continue in the future.[239]

By letter dated October 04, 2009, Dr. Aafia wrote to the court she had relieved Ms. Dawn Cardi and Charles Swift from representing her. She said these attorneys should not be doing anything related to her, and if they had sent anyone overseas or had gone themselves, then all such actions were null and void and should be canceled.[240]

By order dated October 20, 2009, the court ordered it would take up the issue of representation/counsel in the next conference hearing on Nov 03, 2009 at 2:00 pm. The court also ordered it would need 1. Aafia's proposal for who would represent (if not current counsel) on her scheduled trial (Jan 19, 2010 trial) and 2. Suggested allocution(s) from both sides to resolve the counsel issue. It further ordered that both items 1 and 2 were to be submitted (served and filed) by Oct 27, 2009, at noon.[241]

During the November 03, 2009, conference hearing Judge Berman said that most of the conversation today would be on the issue of legal representation of Dr. Aafia. He said for this conversation he would close the courtroom and ask the government to be excluded because attorneys representing Dr. Aafia are going to get into attorney-client privilege area. He also said he needs to know a little bit better from Dr. Aafia and her attorneys about the nature of the problem. Dr. Aafia abruptly pointed to Judge Berman the attorneys' visits were torture for her and if he could please stop them. Judge Berman said he asked attorneys to ascertain whether Dr. Aafia had a proposal for who would represent her at trial. He also said he asked them to submit suggested allocutions or questions to deal with that issue. Dr. Aafia interrupted and said, she had requested last time she would like to speak with the FBI agents, Ms. Mae Syed, and Mr. LaVigne, and the attorneys to her right and left had actively blocked that, and she had a serious problem with that. She said they were quoting Judge Berman as being the cause behind it. On this Judge Berman replied to Dr. Aafia that he was used to that, as people always say it is the judge's fault. Then Judge Berman asked everybody in the courtroom to leave so the defense attorneys and Dr. Aafia could get into ex parte session. Once the proceedings resumed, Judge Berman said he didn't think it was appropriate at the time to make any changes in counsel and the representation and he was not planning to do it today. Dr. Aafia said she didn't want to be in court. Judge Berman said she had the right to be in the court. Dr. Aafia said she understood and appreciated that he was letting her know, but she is willing to give up her right. Judge Berman asked Dr. Aafia if she was willing to give up that right because of the issue of strip search. Dr. Aafia said that was one of the reasons, and she was responsible for the decision also. She said the MDC did have video conferencing arrangements, but she was not allowed to use it. Ms. Sharp told Judge Berman that Dr. Aafia was upset with the court. Mr. LaVigne interjected and submitted to the court the proposed questions that should be asked of Dr. Aafia. He said could the court state as to whether those questions were asked. Dr. Aafia answered Mr. LaVigne that why don't you ask her directly. She is here now, and ask her whatever you want, and she will answer. Ms. Dawn Cardi said to the judge she didn't think it was appropriate for the government to be asking questions about an ex parte conference. Judge Berman answered Mr. LaVigne that he had asked most of the questions the government had submitted during ex parte proceedings, and he didn't want to go into all of those questions again, and based on his findings he was not making any changes to the representation. Mr. LaVigne then said Dr. Aafia needed to be apprised of her rights under the confrontation clause, to sit in person and actually face the witness. Dr. Aafia said she was giving up that right as well, as any other right the court wanted to give her. Judge Berman shared, he had told her she had the right to be in court in every proceeding and to pass a note to her counsel to confer with her counsel on the spot as to how the proceeding was going.

Dr. Aafia said she was giving up that right also, but the strip search was one of the reasons, however, not the only reason. She said if she talked to her attorney, it didn't mean there was an attorney-client relationship. Dr. Aafia then asked Judge Berman that he was not giving her the chance to find another attorney of her own choice. Judge Berman said that was not true; he had asked her during the course of the colloquy whether she had a different plan and different attorneys. Dr. Aafia said, if he had given her some time, she could have found some other attorneys. Judge Berman said that he had always entertained any application she made, but the flipside was there was no alternative plan by Dr. Aafia in retaining new attorneys.[242]

Following the hearing held on November 3, 2009, and based on the record, including the parties' submissions, and the ex parte proceedings on November 3, 2009, the court didn't believe that defense was inhibiting or foreclosing any of Dr. Aafia's legal options. The court said that despite Dr. Aafia's oral and written "complaints" about counsel, there had been no significant breakdown in communication between Dr. Aafia and her counsel and if anything she had exhibited an occasional inclination not to cooperate with her counsel, while counsels appeared to have gone to greater lengths to cooperate with her. Therefore the court found that any change in defense counsel was not required or appropriate at the time.[243]

During the November 19, 2009, conference hearing, Dr. Aafia said to the court she couldn't refuse the attorneys visits as they come and sit at her door and the visits went on for hours and hours and she can't deal with them; it was torture for her. She said that was not the way attorneys were supposed to deal with her. Dr. Aafia said she had requested to remove the attorneys from her door, and also requested not to get video conferencing done because she was boycotting the trial and was not participating in it. She further said she didn't allow anybody to use any statements she had made in her defense. Judge Berman said that for this it was important she was present in court. Dr. Aafia replied it was not important she be in court because it didn't matter. She again requested the judge she didn't want to meet and deal with the attorneys anymore. She said they could come and say whatever they want but she is out of it all, and such visits must not be considered attorney visits, as they were just people coming at her door and talking. Judge Berman said attorneys were people, too. Dr. Aafia said she understood that attorneys are people and she was also a person.[244]

On the January 11, 2010, conference hearing the government arraigned Dr. Aafia. Ms. Dawn Cardi said Dr. Aafia entered a plea of not guilty. Dr. Aafia intervened and said they were not her attorneys and she had fired them many times. Judge Berman said, "Aafia I am not going to have a big fight with you." Dr. Aafia said, "Then take me out." Judge Berman replied he was speaking and she could speak on her turn. Dr. Aafia again said to Judge Berman he never gave her a turn, and those were not her attorneys. She said she had boycotted the trial and it was an international crime and against international law. Judge Berman said she could include that in the record and the reporter would include it in the court record.[245]

During the January 13, 2010 conference hearing Dr. Aafia said she was only quiet because she didn't agree with all that was happening. She said it was all lies, hypocrisy, and injustice, and she was just in the court because she had been forced to be in court. Dr. Aafia said she relieved her attorneys once again from whatever they were doing. She also said she wanted to make it clear that if she was quite then, that was not taken as her consent to whatever was going on. She said it was the exact opposite of what she wanted, and being quiet was the most peaceful protest she could make to fight all the injustice that was being done to her in her name. Judge Berman said that Dr. Aafia should know her statements were always included in the record and would be done for that day as well. Dr. Aafia said she was not sure if she agreed with what Judge Berman was saying he always did because she hadn't seen what was included in the record.

Judge Berman said her lawyers could show it to her. Dr. Aafia again said she was not in touch with the lawyers because they were not her lawyers, and she didn't know what they were doing and she was not part of it all. Judge Berman replied to Dr. Aafia that the court had talked about her representation many times, and he would stand on the record of their previous discussions, which was that he thought attorneys who were in the court were appropriately in court on behalf of the defense. Dr. Aafia said not on her behalf. Judge Berman said he understood she disagreed with that, but certainly, there was an opportunity for lawyers of her choice. Dr. Aafia said she was never given an opportunity to get her lawyers. Judge Berman said "Ok, well we have a respectful disagreement about that."[246]

On January 19, 2010, before the commencement of trial hearing Judge Berman told Dr. Aafia he needed to have a conversation with her and wanted to ask her a series of questions. He said first he wanted to know if she knew she had the right to be present at any and all phases of the criminal trial. Dr. Aafia said she thought there was a difference between rights and being forced to come to court. She said they had to strip her and she had a problem with that and the whole world knew that, too. Judge Berman again asked about did she understand that she had the right to be in court. Dr. Aafia said she didn't need to take that right and she was being forced to come to court; she rather preferred to stay in the prison cell. She again said she was boycotting the trial. Judge Berman then asked Dr. Aafia that did she understand she had the right to work with her attorneys at all phases of the criminal trial and to consult with them. Dr. Aafia replied she didn't accept those attorneys as her attorneys, and they were imposed on her by Judge Berman.

Judge Berman asked Dr. Aafia that there was a written waiver document her attorneys presented to her, and was it true she refused to sign that document? Dr. Aafia said she had a problem with what her attorneys had written on it. Judge Berman then asked Dr. Aafia about whether she had signed it. Dr. Aafia said 'no.' She shared the way they had written it and the way it was phrased, it was like she was being asked to give up everything, and gaining nothing. She said she would be forced to come to court by just signing it. Judge Berman asked Dr. Aafia that did she understand she had the right to be outside of the courtroom even if she was otherwise directed to be outside for prayer? Dr. Aafia said she checked the prayer time by looking outside from the courtroom window, and she didn't need to ask anybody for any favors. Judge Berman asked Dr. Aafia that did she know the option he was providing her was that if she were not in the courtroom then she would be in a holding cell outside the courtroom with a TV monitor. Dr. Aafia said she didn't understand why she couldn't be in prison cell where the MDC could make arrangements for video conference. She said why didn't the court accept her boycott and let her just stay in the prison cell. Judge Berman said she had two options.

Either she was welcome to be in court for all the phases of the proceeding or she would be in the prison cell with the TV monitor and with access to her attorneys, including one of the attorneys who would sit out there with her. Dr. Aafia said that was the biggest problem, that the attorneys sat in her prison cell and kept talking and saying things to her she didn't want to hear. Judge Berman said that did Dr. Aafia understand she didn't have the right to disrupt the proceedings and to speak out of turn. Dr. Aafia said she never got a turn and when she did, she got scratched. Judge Berman said that based on the attorney's submissions he planned to gesture as unobtrusively as possible, although he thought it would be difficult sometimes, as he might have to make some verbal statements and comments in order to control the courtroom and the proceedings. He said he had planned to advise the jury that they should disregard Dr. Aafia's outbursts and not hold them against her and similarly her absence or absences should not be held against her either. Dr. Aafia said she was getting negativity from everywhere and she couldn't even say a single word. She said they had accused her of anti-Semitism. She said she felt everything was a lie and she was boycotting the trial. Judge Berman then asked Dr. Aafia if she wished to be present in court that day for the trial or would she waive her right to be present. She said if she had the right to not be in court, then she should be in her prison cell. Judge Berman asked her again that did she wish to be in court that day for the trial or does she waive her right to be present. Dr. Aafia said both options were unacceptable. Judge Berman said that he would take that as not a waiver of her right and he would take it as an indicator of her wish to be present. Dr. Aafia then said the press needed to talk to her as she couldn't work with the agencies, and she had been trying to talk to media and it was her last opportunity before she got sentenced. She said it was important and she must not be ignored for the sake of God and for this beautiful country. She also asked to make her written documents public, the whole document, so the world and especially Americans could see exactly what she was saying. Dr. Aafia said she didn't want bits and pieces pulled out of context as she was not anti any religion or any race, etc. She further said somebody was using Americans as a tool to fight their war.[247]

During the second day of the trial hearing, dated January 20, 2009, Judge Berman notified that Dr. Aafia had the right but not an obligation to testify for the defense. Dr. Aafia said she would like to testify. Judge Berman said off course she could, but she needed to talk to her attorneys about how and when. Dr. Aafia said they were not her attorneys and she never accepted them for a day. She said she relieved them again from their services. She also told Judge Berman he forced her to come to court and she never got her turn to say anything. Judge Berman said that every defendant in every criminal case had the right but not an obligation to testify. Dr. Aafia replied the defendant had the right and obligation not to be present in court. Judge Berman said that if she opted to testify it would not be when she wanted to speak, as there was an appropriate circumstance after the government had concluded its case. He further said that usually more often the defendant's testimony is the subject of conversation between the defendant and their attorneys. Dr. Aafia said she didn't have a defense team and they were not her attorneys. Judge Berman then told Dr. Aafia that she had no right to disrupt the proceedings and to speak out of turn. Dr. Aafia said she understood that nobody had the right to force her out of her cell and bring her to the court building and then give her all kinds of unacceptable options. She said she had boycotted this trial and she was happy to remain in her prison cell. Judge Berman asked Dr. Aafia if she was happy to remain in the cell. She said she meant her prison cell. Dr. Aafia then told Judge Berman he was taking her rights away. Judge Berman said he didn't intend to get into any more debates with her.

He said he controlled the proceedings and it was his responsibility to keep order in the courtroom; she must understand she must not disrupt the proceedings and speak out of turn. Dr. Aafia said she understood English and she understood what Judge Berman was saying. Dr. Aafia then told Ms. Sharp she could speak for herself. She then said she had objections on many things but since she had boycotted the trial, that is why she was quiet. She was also not planning to defend herself on the shooting charges the prosecution had made against her. She also said she didn't agree with the victim being put on trial in an illegal country. Judge Berman then said that she couldn't interrupt, and couldn't have outbursts because it won't be considered testimony. And if that happened, then she would be excluded from the courtroom, and she would be asked to sit in the cell adjacent to the courtroom, where there would be a TV monitor and one of her attorneys maybe Ms. Sharp could be present. Dr. Aafia said she didn't want such a setting, and she didn't look or even talk to her lawyers; she didn't want them either. She said they are respected people, but they are not representing her. She said she didn't understand why the court didn't let her just stay in her prison cell. She again said she had tons of pro-American writings and she had expressed her feelings in those writings, and how none of them have been mentioned in the court. Judge Berman said he wanted Dr. Aafia to understand the four attorneys were retained by the Government of Pakistan for her. Dr. Aafia replied he is insisting her to keep them when she had already relieved them. Judge Berman said CJA attorneys have been appointed by him for her. Dr. Aafia said she has relieved them many times, and they were respectably working for others but not for her. Judge Berman said they had gone through many times in the past about representation. Dr. Aafia replied "so." Judge Berman said she was given every opportunity to decide about representation. Dr. Aafia said she wasn't given any chance, and she was at Carswell when all the decisions about representation had taken place. Judge Berman said she had been treated no differently than any other prisoner who came to that court. She said she disagreed and was going to be quiet, but that didn't mean she agreed with everything. Judge Berman said to Dr. Aafia that he would not tolerate any outbursts or speaking out. Dr. Aafia replied she made no outbursts and was just talking.[248]

On the January 25, 2010, trial hearing Dr. Aafia was removed from the courtroom by Judge Berman due to her outbursts. The defense then made an application with respect to the additional security measures that had been taken during the course of the trial. Ms. Moreno said that some time ago the US Marshals escorted Dr. Aafia to the lockup in full view of the jurors, and the Marshals were quite physical with Dr. Aafia during that maneuver. Therefore, the defense moved for a mistrial. She said that kind of conduct denigrates the presumption of innocence in front of the jury. Judge Berman said that Ms. Moreno's application was respectfully denied and said it is more than common knowledge her client Dr. Aafia had been disruptive in the courtroom. He said that one big responsibility he had was to make sure the proceeding was orderly and he had advised Dr. Aafia that she had the obligation not to be disorderly and/or disruptive. He also added that nevertheless she had been persistent in being disruptive, and it was entirely appropriate for her to be escorted out of the courtroom when she acted out. Judge Berman further said it would in fact be helpful if the defense could spend more time with Dr. Aafia and engrain in her the protocols she must follow. Ms. Moreno said Dr. Aafia didn't communicate with the defense counsel. She said Dr. Aafia didn't talk to them. She also shared that just that day she went to meet Dr. Aafia. She tried to speak to Dr. Aafia to explain some things to her. She indicated that Dr. Aafia said that if she didn't leave immediately, she would accuse her of harassment. Judge Berman said it was just his observation and he didn't mean to dispute or refute her, and that he had seen Dr. Aafia conferring with Ms. Sharp on many occasions, including during the trial. Dr. Aafia then interjected and said to Judge Berman she respectfully states he was lying about everything he said. The Judge said if there was anything else she wanted to say, and she said no she just had to say that.[249]

Chapter 8

Verdict, Sentencing, And Dr. Aafia

*T*HE VERDICT AND SENTENCING OF DR. AAFIA have caused a global controversy. In other to give you the facts about what happened and how such a conclusion was reached, here I present in detail the jury verdict, Judge Berman concluding remarks and Dr. Aafia's speech during the sentencing hearing.

On February 3, 2010, the jury reached a verdict. The Deputy Clerk asked the Foreperson to stand up and asked how the jury was found as to the following questions:

THE DEPUTY CLERK: Question One, Count one: Attempted murder of United States Nationals?

THE FOREPERSON: Guilty

THE DEPUTY CLERK: Please indicate whether the defendant also committed the crime with premeditation

---

THE FOREPERSON: No

THE DEPUTY CLERK: Question Two, Count Two: Attempted murder of United States officers and employees?

THE FOREPERSON: Guilty

THE DEPUTY CLERK: Please indicate whether the defendant also committed this crime with premeditation

---

THE FOREPERSON: No

THE DEPUTY CLERK: Question Three, Count Three: Armed assault of United States officers and employees?

THE FOREPERSON: Guilty

THE DEPUTY CLERK: Question Four, Count Four: Using and carrying a firearm during and in relation to a crime of violence?

THE FOREPERSON: Guilty

THE DEPUTY CLERK: Question Five, Count Five: Assault of United States officers and employees, assault of Interpreter One Ahmad Gul?

THE FOREPERSON: Guilty

THE DEPUTY CLERK: Question Six, Count Six: Assault of United States officers and employees, assault of Special Agent One, Erik Negron?

THE FOREPERSON: Guilty

THE DEPUTY CLERK: Question Seven, Count Seven: Assault of United States officers and employees, assault of US Army Officer two, Captain Snyder?

THE FOREPERSON: Guilty

THE DEPUTY CLERK: All jurors polled; verdict unanimous[250]

The sentencing hearing was set on September 23, 2010. Judge Berman said it was a complicated trial, not necessarily because of the charges in the indictment but because of the issues that were sometimes peripheral to the charges. He said there were security issues which needed to be attended to as done in high profile cases. He said despite precautions there was a serious incident in court in which a member of the audience allegedly made inappropriate and threatening gestures to two jurors which, after questioning the jurors, caused him to excuse two jurors and replace them with alternates and to exclude the audience member from further proceedings. It also caused him to refer the matter to the United States Attorney's Office where it was pending. He further said there was the issue of Dr. Aafia's outbursts in the courtroom in front of the prospective jurors during the trial. He said these caused the government to request the defendant be excluded from the trial and try the case without her. Judge Berman said he concluded that was not a good idea and he denied the request. He said it would have made no sense, in his view, to arrest a non-US, in this case, a Pakistani citizen, in Afghanistan and transport her to New York City for trial and then conduct a trial in her absence even though she was the cause of the disruption.

Judge Berman further said that every day of the trial Dr. Aafia was given the opportunity to be in the courtroom and conduct herself appropriately, which she clearly knew how to do. He said when she was disruptive, which did happen from time to time, we made adjustments such as removing her to a cell adjacent to the courtroom where a TV has been installed and where she could still, together with her attorneys such as Ms. Sharp, view and listen to all the proceedings. He said there was never a single moment when Dr. Aafia was denied the opportunity to confront her accusers or when she didn't have the opportunity to participate in her defense in a public trial. He said Dr. Aafia engaged in the trial proceedings over the objections of her attorneys and following a hearing on January 28, 2010, Dr. Aafia elected to take the stand in her defense which was her right under the legal system.

Judge Berman concluded there was insufficient evidence in the record to conclusively confirm all of her whereabouts between the years 2003 and 2008. He said it had not been established definitively why she and her son were in Afghanistan in 2008. He said speculations had ranged from the following; one, that she was looking for Ammar Al Baluchi, who he understood, she was married to and who has been held along with his uncle Khalid Sheikh Mohammed at the United States Base in Guantanamo Bay on terror-related charges. The Judge said the other speculation was she was on a mission to attack Americans. Another speculation was she was there to distribute documents instructing the Taliban how to make explosives to destroy the foreigners and the government army.

He said the court also noted that Dr. Aafia was an unindicted co-conspirator in the case of *The United States of America v Uzair Paracha*. He said the government, in this case, noted that the charges that are the seven counts against her for which she was indicted and convicted were not related to the conspiracy at issue in the *Uzair Paracha* case.[251]

He said in considering these seven counts for sentencing under the sentencing law, he considered, count One, Two, Three and Five, Six, and Seven as a group, and considered count Four separately which, by law, needed to be sentenced consecutively.

Judge Berman said that the upshot of his analysis was that a sentence of significant incarceration was called for in the case. He said he had been through the sentencing analysis, and it was complicated and somewhat technical, but the conclusion, that significant incarceration was appropriate seemed (to him) completely obvious and indeed compelled by the jury verdict and the relevant factors under the sentencing law 18, United States Code, Section 3553(a).

Judge Berman finally said the total punishment would be 76 years on six counts; One, Two, Three, Five, Six and Seven; 20 years on Count One, 20 years on Count Two, 20 years on Count Three, with respect to Count Five he thought it would be eight years. With respect to Count Six and Seven he thought they would be Four years each. He said he had distinguished somewhat between the assault against interpreter Gul who fought with Dr. Aafia vigorously to subdue her while she held on to an M4 rifle, and jeopardized his life and those against Captain Snyder and Agent Negron, with whom Dr. Aafia struggled forcibly but after the weapon had been taken from her. He said with respect to Count Four, he also intended to impose a 10-year sentence which, under the law must run consecutively. He concluded the total would be a sentence of 86 years of incarceration.[252]

Judge Berman also recommended Dr. Aafia be housed again at FMC Carswell in Texas, where she was housed before. He also recommended she be given periodic assessments for mental health and help in any follow-up treatments, therapy or medication that may be recommended.[253]

Judge Berman then asked Dr. Aafia if she would like to be heard. Dr. Aafia said she had not taken any notes or anything, but she didn't know she will get a chance to speak as she had planned to sleep while in the courtroom. She said she is fine with it and thanks God. She said she wants to touch on a few things that were mentioned. She said there are many things she didn't agree with which are not true, but she is going to touch on the things which would affect, in her opinion, the lives of a lot of people. She said it is not of crucial importance to her where she spends the rest of her life because she doesn't believe that Judge Berman or others, or even herself was in charge of this, other than God. She said she was not being tortured in prison at MDC as was being spread amongst the Muslims and she had a big problem with that because it is a lie. She said such issues are emotionally disturbing for people overseas and she didn't want people to be misinformed overseas about her case, because they knew she was innocent. Dr. Aafia said she didn't agree with any of the charges against her, but she was going to go over that. She said people sent her cards, sympathy letters; they were all strangers. She said her brother sent her a card too asking how she was, but she never replied to any of the posts.

She said she tried to send three letters from the MDC, and one of them was returned. She said one of the letters she had sent was certified with a return receipt, but she never received a return receipt, so she assumed that MDC never sent it. Dr. Aafia said she has understood through some information that Chief of Intelligence at MDC, Mr. Desmond was responsible for all of that. She said she had very credible information which she wanted to give to the FBI, but the MDC didn't let her. She said Mr. Desmond is the man involved in planning attacks against the US and she had a lot of information about it. She said she appreciated Judge Berman that he did quote what she wrote to him through letters. She said she was not against Israel and for the Sake of God she was not against anybody. She said there was an issue, and she was forcefully brought to this country. Dr. Aafia shared there were people who were assigned to do all kinds of crazy and ridiculous things to her so they could make a big war, and it was part of the whole game. She said she had a background of being a social worker. She said her mother was a social worker and she was her assistant. She said he had a lot of experience in social work.

Dr. Aafia said she had to mention certain things sometimes and had mentioned the state of Israel many times. She said people could call it a political statement, but it wasn't one as it had nothing to do with politics; it was a humanitarian problem. She said if the State of Israel wanted to fight a war, then they should fight it themselves. She said they shouldn't misinform the Americans and make them fight what they didn't want to fight. Dr. Aafia said she was kept in a secret prison and no one wanted to acknowledge it, but she was not getting into that discussion at such a point. She shared she wasn't paranoid and wasn't mentally ill.

She said people who are causing trouble between countries on a grand scale must be genetically tested because they hide their identity and that was the problem. She said it was easily verifiable and all they needed was to do a simple DNA test to check the pedigree of a person.

Dr. Aafia said most of her teeth are not her own as she got beaten many times by her captors in Afghanistan. She shared she was given artificial teeth, and sometimes they fall off while she is talking, but she manages to eat. She said she was sent to Ghazni by her captors for a mission and that mission was never successful. Furthermore, she shared said she never understood her captor's mission but she was messed up and she didn't know what happened. She said she did all of that because they said they would give her back her children. She was only thinking about her children at the time.

Dr. Aafia said she had a good relationship with some Israelis and she shared she definitely believed there was a certain element among them who were making big wars. She said she had worked with war victims in Bosnia and recently she was given a book at the MDC about the Burundi and Rwanda conflict and how one survivor escaped. She said it was a wonderful book, but the massacre was really heart wrenching. Dr. Aafia shared said she truly didn't like wars.

She said she did send a letter to the Dallas Peace Center because they sent her a newsletter through mail at MDC. She said she only wrote a letter to them because she thought there was somebody who is lobbying for the truth and didn't want war. Dr. Aafia said that a lot of things were attempted on her at MDC and the bosses at MDC didn't even know them, but God protected her so why would she complain. She said she would not say if her experience at FMC Carswell was better or worse, but it was definitely different from MDC, but she didn't complain, and was happy, all thanks to God.

Dr. Aafia said it was not correct to say she was not cooperating or talking with the psychologists' department in MDC. She said most of the psychologists lied because they were paid big money. She said if she knew they were honest, then she might have talked to them. Dr.Kemky, whom she wished was in front of her in the courtroom, told her she had post-traumatic stress disorder. She said Dr. Kemky was a weak but a very good person. Kemky told her she was under tremendous pressure and not to say what she believed in. But she said she would say what she had to in court.

Dr. Aafia shared she didn't blame Dr. Kemky for saying she had post-traumatic stress disorder because she did have it. She said that if you had been tortured in prison for many years, then PTSD would trigger, but that didn't make a person mentally insane. She said she didn't have it at the present moment and thanked God for that.

She said she disagreed with the defense she was mentally ill; in fact, she was not mentally sick at all. She said, "Schizophrenia, no way on earth excuse me." Dr. Aafia said anybody who had attended the trial and heard her testify can bear witness to that she was not mentally sick.

She said again she wasn't anti-Israel but, yes she had said they masterminded 9/11 and she had proof of that, too. She said she was saying again that there were attacks being planned against America; big wars being planned and the Israelis were involved in it. She said she told them to stop it and not to do it. Dr. Aafia said America really needed to wake up to their domestic problems.

She said she was not allowed to talk to the FBI for three months and she begged everybody at MDC for allowing her to talk to the FBI. She said if she was a criminal, would she have ever requested to speak with the FBI? She said she is saying again in front of everyone (that day) that she wanted to talk to the FBI. Dr. Aafia said Angela Sercer, who came to court for the trial proceedings and who was with her at Bagram, never told her she was an FBI agent.

She said she regurgitated what her captives fed her when she was in the secret prison because she thought it was a game to get her children back, but it was a plot. She said they did brainwashing and she had discussed all of that with the psychologists.

Dr. Aafia said she didn't want 9/11, and she didn't want any bloodshed. She said she wanted to make peace and end wars. She said anyone could have conveyed this to President Obama because he was serious about peace, but no one conveyed her message.

She said she wanted to share something with all the people sitting in the courtroom, and that would shock Muslims, but she didn't mean any disrespect. She said if she were under oath, she would put her hand on the Holy book and would say she is a Muslim and she loves America too; there is no harm in it. Dr. Aafia said she loves Zambia too because that was also her homeland. She said she loves the whole world and had no problem with all races and all of its people. She said God wanted her to survive and she knew it is for a good reason.

Dr. Aafia shared her dream in the courtroom in which she said she saw Prophet Muhammad (Peace Be upon Him) and it was shortly after the trial. She said before going to sleep she was thinking and wishing somebody could tell the Taliban in Afghanistan that Prophet Muhammad (Peace Be upon Him) called mercy on the entire universe, the war in Afghanistan was a misunderstanding, and it should end. She said she was also thinking of Yvonne Ridley, a journalist who had been working on her case. She said then she went to sleep and saw in her dream Prophet Muhammad (Peace Be upon Him) entered the room. The room was full of American soldiers, who were sitting on the floor hands behind their back, apparently like prisoners of war. She said she was following the Prophet in that room; then she said the Prophet walked through to another room next to it, and that room was also full of American soldiers. They were also sitting with hands behind their back. She said she was following the Prophet and then he turned to the soldiers. He addressed them in English. He said only one sentence, she didn't remember the exact words but he was consoling them, his tone was gentle and talked of forgiveness and mercy.

She said this dream gave her peace, and she realized God had heard her and accepted her efforts. He was telling her He is sending His mercy to all mankind. She said Muslims might think, 'what on Earth?' Those people were killing Muslims. How could the Prophet console them?

She said American soldiers don't know what they are doing and she kept saying this. She said there had been American soldiers who were nice to her in the prisons at Carswell and the MDC, and she had cried for them. She said she prayed to God to save their lives. Dr. Aafia said she didn't want to name them, because she didn't want anyone hurting them, but she really loved them because they didn't even know why they were sent to Afghanistan. She said the Israeli Americans kept her daughter for years and they didn't rape her; they didn't sexually abuse her. She said she was not sad, she was not distressed, and she was well in prison, and she thanked God.

She shared again that Yvonne Ridley was captured in Afghanistan by the Taliban. She said they treated her well and released her and then she became a Muslim. She said she wears a headscarf and she still did her work and everything. She said Yvonne Ridley was very impressed by the way the Taliban treated her.

Dr. Aafia said you people don't know what a mother goes through when she is missing her children. People would not understand unless they experience it. She said there were thousands and thousands of children in prison all over the world. She said she couldn't imagine what their mothers were going through. Furthermore, she said she had a six-month-old son, who was sick and she didn't know whether he survived. If her older two survived then he might have, too. She said she was appealing to all governments holding prisoners that for God's sake stop it. She said she knew there were many Palestinian children in Israeli prisons because they threw a stone at the soldiers. Dr. Aafia she said they were just kids, too.

She requested everyone not to lobby for her but to do something for the kids and for other prisoners. She advised Muslims not to commit any act of violence, not to get emotional, and just pray to God. She further requested Muslims living in non-Muslim countries anywhere in the world to teach people about Islam. Dr. Aafia said people needed to know about Islam and they needed to know the Prophet (Peace Be Upon Him) is a Prophet sent as a mercy to the universe.[254]

She said she remembered very clearly from the trial time the instructions given to the jury. She said all the jurymen were American, and she said she was informed by one of the attorneys the jury would give a non-guilty verdict, but then the verdict changed.

She said there is a verse in the Quran and it is Surah Hujuraat verse No. 6 or 7, which meant that if you get news from a source which is not trustworthy, verify it. She said this verse was very important in her case. Dr. Aafia said there were many rumors in the case and pretty much all of facts were not true. She advised Muslims that if they hear anything about her being tortured in prison, they must verify it through verifiable means as she didn't want violence in her name. She said in prison people came to her and asked her how she coped with anger and how she was so happy after the verdict. That answer she always told them was that God had put contentment in her heart. She said whatever God had given her she was happy because she believed God is the only one in charge.

She said God showed her dreams which she never used to have before. She said she saw Prophet Jesus (Peace Be upon Him) in her dream, too. The dream was very long. So, she didn't want to go into all of the details. She said she had encountered many Christians and she had talked a lot about religion with them. They were very good people. She said there was always an agreement in their debates and very little disagreement. There was a lot of room for constructive talk.

She said to believe her that when God wrote for her to come out of prison, she would come out. She said she was kept in a secret prison for years, and people thought she was dead, but she stayed alive because it was written for her that way by God. She said she was content and thanks Allah.[255]

Dr. Aafia said Prophet Muhammad (Peace Be upon Him) forgave all his personal enemies no matter how unjust they were toward him. She said we all know how much he suffered, but he never took personal revenge, ever. Dr. Aafia appealed to Muslims to forgive everyone connected to her case. She said if she is forgiving them, then they should, too. She said she forgave the two soldiers who shot her. She said the world is full of injustices, and we could strive in many ways to make the world a more livable peaceful place. Dr. Aafia said she had also forgiven Judge Berman.[256]

Judge Berman told her she had the right to appeal the sentence and if she was unable to pay the cost of an appeal she had the right to apply for leave to appeal in forma pauperis. He said if she requests, the Clerk of the court would prepare and file a notice of appeal on her behalf immediately.

Dr. Aafia answered that the way the trial was handled the appeal she assumes would be the same and under those kind of circumstances where she couldn't get the attorneys of her choice. She said she was dumped by people who were not authorized on her behalf. Furthermore, she said she didn't want anybody to spend a penny toward her appeal. She said it was useless, pointless, and a waste of time, energy and money. She said she appealed to God as He hears her. Judge Berman said she could take some time to reconsider her decision. Dr. Aafia again said she didn't want to appeal. She said she went to MIT and the government labeled her as mental and many other things. She said she was at the Harvard of Israel and now she is at the MIT of Israel, meaning Manhattan Institute of Theater Arts.

Ms. Dawn Cardi said, "Your Honor, she will file a notice of Appeal, and they will work out what will happen." Dr. Aafia interrupted and said, "nothing on her behalf and please stay away from her life." Ms. Dawn Cardi said she was actually obliged as CJA counsel to file Dr. Aafia's notice of appeal and then they could figure out what would happen. Dr. Aafia said 'no' again, and strongly refused this counsel or any other appointed by anyone or self-appointed. She further said she would take Ms. Dawn Cardi to court one day. Judge Berman then asked if anyone wanted to add anything to that day's proceeding. Everyone replied with a 'no.' Judge Berman told Dr. Aafia that it had been a long day, and he wished her the very best going forward.[257]

Chapter 9

§ 2255 Motion To Vacate & Motion To Recuse The Court

*T*HE MOTION TO VACATE, SET ASIDE OR COR-
rect a sentence provided by 28 U.S.C. § 2255 is a modern
descendant of the common law petition for a writ of habeas
corpus. It is available only to people convicted in federal
courts and are in custody. The § 2255 motion is the post-conviction tool
most federal prisoners turn to after they have exhausted their appeals. In
the US judicial system, it is a powerful tool to right injustices that were
not or could not have been raised on direct appeal. This is because it gives
courts broad discretion in fashioning appropriate relief, including dis-
missal of all charges and release of the prisoner, retrial, or resentencing.

On May 12, 2014, Dr. Aafia filed the MOTION TO VACATE
SENTENCE PURSUANT TO 28 U.S.C. § 2255 and a separate MOTION
TO RECUSE THE COURT through her retained attorneys Ms. Tina Foster
and Robert J.Boyle.

Dr. Aafia filed a motion pursuant to 28 U.S.C. § 2255 to vacate a
judgment of the Southern District of New York dated September 23, 2010,
under Indictment 08-CR-826 convicting Dr. Aafia of attempted murder

of United States nationals in violation of 18 U.S.C. § 2332(b); attempted murder of United States Officer and employees in violation of 18 U.S.C. § 1114; armed assault of United States officers and employees in violation of 18 U.S.C. § 111(b); discharging of a firearm during a crime of violence in violation of 18 U.S.C. § 924(c); assaulting United States officers and employees in violation of 18 U.S.C. § 111(a).

The claims made in the motion were as follow:

1. Aafia was denied her right to counsel as guaranteed by the Sixth Amendment when the court permitted her to be represented by counsel retained by a third party where she didn't assent to that representation

2. Aafia was denied to her right to counsel as guaranteed by the Sixth Amendment when she was denied a meaningful opportunity to obtain and retain counsel of her own choice

3. Aafia was denied her right to counsel as guaranteed by the Sixth Amendment due to a complete breakdown in the attorney-client relationship between Aafia and all counsel

4. Aafia was denied her right to counsel as guaranteed by the Sixth Amendment where counsel operated under potential and/or actual conflict of interest due to the fact that they were being paid by the third party

5. Aafia was denied her right to effective assistance of trial counsel as guaranteed by the Sixth Amendment when her attorneys:

   a. Failed to investigate the circumstances surrounding her disappearance in 2003

   b. Failed to utilize, during cross-examination of the government's witness, the video showing that the holes in the walls were present before the July 18, 2008 shooting incident

   c. Failed to object to the prosecutor's improper remarks during opening and rebuttal summation and/or move for a mistrial

d. Failed to move for a new trial pursuant to Fed. R. Crim. P 33 when they learned of the recording wherein a Pakistani law enforcement official admitted participation in Aafia's 2003 abduction and subsequent detention

6. Aafia was denied her right to effective assistance of appellate counsel as guaranteed by the Sixth Amendment when her attorneys failed to argue that plain error was committed during the prosecutor summations

7. Aafia was denied due process of law when the prosecution failed to produce evidence in its possession that would have proven that she was abducted in 2003 and after that turned over to United States custody[258]

Dr. Aafia also filed a MOTION TO RECUSE Judge Berman from presiding over the instant 28 U.S.C. § 2255 motion proceeding and for random reassignment to a different judge. Mr. Boyle, Dr. Aafia's attorney, sought the motion to recuse the Court, pursuant to United States Code, Section 455(a), (b)(1) and (b)(5)(iv). He argued principally that an objective observer would question Judge Berman's impartiality on issues raised in the Section 2255 motion, because on January 27, 2010, Mr. Husain Haqqani, the then-ambassador of Pakistan to the United States and the person who retained attorneys for Dr. Aafia, over Dr. Aafia's objections, was present in the court, and Judge Berman met with him prior to the start of the day's proceedings. Upon information and belief, none of the parties were present during Judge Berman meeting with Ambassador Haqqani, and Judge Berman has knowledge of disputed facts and might be called as material witness. Mr. Boyle further added that Dr. Aafia always believed the government of Pakistan was responsible for her 2003 abduction and further believed they were not acting in her best interests in her criminal case when they hired the defense counsel.[259]

On May 20, 2014, the court directed attorney Boyle to present written documentation that he had been retained by Dr. Aafia to represent her.[260] In response, Mr. Boyle relied upon the letter dated October 3, 2013, from Dr. Aafia which stated "Please be advised that I have retained Tina Foster as my attorney to represent me in the US courts."[261]

Mr. Boyle also relied upon the transcript of his phone conversation with Dr. Aafia mentioned in his letter of declaration to the court dated May 27, 2014. In this letter, he stated that "On May 5, 2014, he participated in an unmonitored legal telephone call arranged through FMC Carswell, where Dr. Aafia is incarcerated. Ms. Tina Foster and a person who identified herself as Dr. Aafia both also participated in the telephone call. He identified himself to Dr. Aafia. The conversation lasted approximately one hour. He took contemporaneous notes. Near the end of the call, he and Ms. Tina foster specifically asked Dr. Aafia whether she should authorize him and Ms. Tina Foster to file the 28 U.S.C. § 2255 motion on her behalf. She responded affirmatively."[262]

Mr. Boyle also relied upon Dr. Aafia letter to Tina Foster dated May 21, 2014, in which Dr. Aafia stated "To whom it may concern: I confirm that: I have authorized attorneys Tina Foster and Robert Boyle to file a legal case on my behalf, specifically section 2255 motion to vacate and related fillings."[263]

During the July 8, 2014 court hearing, Judge Berman said the purpose of the day's hearing was to resolve the recusal motion filed by Dr. Aafia. Judge Berman said the court deputy was advised on January 26, 2010, by Dr. Aafia's counsel that Hussain Haqqani wished to attend the trial proceedings and expected to come to court on January 27, 2010. Judge Berman said he did not know the ambassador beforehand and had never spoken to him before. He said the ambassador did appear in the courtroom in the morning very shortly before the court proceedings began on January 27, 2010, and his appearance coincided with the then imminent conclusion of the government's case presentation. He said in fact when the trial resumed at or about 9:30 or 9:35 that morning, one stipulation was read by the government and the government then rested. The Judge said he greeted Ambassador Haqqani in the open courtroom and the robing room and not in chambers, for no more than a minute or two, entirely as a courtesy to a foreign dignitary. Judge Berman said he and the ambassador spoke English and exchanged pleasantries such as "a pleasure to meet you." Judge Berman said he told the ambassador he was welcome to be in the courtroom, which was open to the public. Judge Berman said he told the Ambassador a seat had been reserved for him, and they would begin the case at approximately 9:30. He would be free to stay and observe the trial as long as he wished, and that he would also be free to leave the courtroom if he wished to do so. Judge Berman said at no time did he discuss the merits of the case, nor did he discuss, quoting from Mr. Boyle's language, "the process leading up to the retainer agreement" between Pakistan and the three attorneys, nor "any concerns about Aafia rejection of the hired counsel, her mental status, and/or Aafia's stated belief that the attorneys were representing the government of Pakistan's interests and not her own," from Mr. Boyle's submission.

Judge Berman said after that brief meeting with Ambassador Haqqani he returned to the courtroom and commenced the trial proceedings and placed the following on the record, quoting:

> *"Good morning, everybody. Please be seated. So let me just start by saying that we have with us in the audience today Ambassador Haqqani from Pakistan to the United States. I had a brief opportunity to meet him and to welcome him to the courtroom. We acknowledge your presence, and you are very welcome here in this Court."*

Judge Berman said no objection was raised by the defense attorney and he resumed the trial at approximately 9:30, and Ambassador Haqqani left the courtroom sometime prior to the 11:32 recess. Judge Berman said he had not seen or heard from the Ambassador since then. Judge Berman said there was no real or objectively reasonable relationship between his greeting the ambassador on January 27, 2010, and the retainer agreement described by Mr. Boyle and the approval given to three attorneys to assist Ms. Cardi in September 2009. Judge Berman said the Court's greeting of a foreign dignitary in the case didn't and couldn't reasonably have any influence on the court's case determinations and/or the proceedings before it. The Court's goal throughout the case was to conduct all proceedings fairly, efficiently and transparently. Judge Berman concluded that based on the foregoing, the motion submitted by Mr. Boyle for recusal was denied.[264]

On July 2, 2014, Dr. Aafia wrote directly to the court that she hereby withdraws her 2255 application and all related fillings. She also stated Robert J. Boyle was no longer representing her in anything. She said she didn't want to participate in a system of total injustice where she had been punished and tortured repeatedly, without her having committed any crime. Dr. Aafia said she couldn't delude herself into thinking the same element who gave her 86 years for Captain Snyder shooting her, and almost killing her, would give her justice. She said Mr. Boyle gave her a different impression that he could get her out diplomatically without even a treaty, so she agreed to file this 2255 as per his advice. She said that since she has found that the reality is contrary to that impression. She was withdrawing her motion 2255 and all related fillings.[265]

By order dated October 4, 2014, the court dismissed Dr. Aafia's petition while stating that the letter from her dated July 2, 2014, clearly and unequivocally withdrew her § 2255 application and rejected the representation of her by Mr. Boyle. The court also said assume for an argument, that it had been necessary to reach the merits of the 2255 application, i.e., if Aafia had not withdrawn it, the court would likely have denied the application.[266]

Chapter 10

Conclusion — Where Does Dr. Aafia's Case Go From Here?

ONDERING WHAT WILL HAPPEN, IF ANY-thing can happen, with regards to Dr. Aafia Siddiqui's case is a valid thought to have.

Is she innocent? Should she remain behind bars?

Many of you might have already made up your minds about how she should be dealt with.

I have tried my best to present factual information to help you make an informed decision regarding Dr. Aafia's case. I hope that you, after reading it all, can better understand why some believe her to be innocent while others brand her as a terrorist.

You might have noticed certain things too. Namely how there is a lot of classified information being held by the US government and how Judge Berman, even though some argue he could have, decided not to go for the specific classified information while handling this case.

Some believe there were secret negotiations between the defense attorneys, the prosecution and the Judge over what classified information should be released for the purposes of the trial, and an appropriate resolution was achieved which people aren't allowed to know about.

Furthermore, this book talked about the bag which was found when Dr. Aafia was taken into custody in Afghanistan. Many believe the bag with incriminating documents was planted on her by her captors to make her appear as a terrorist.

Some say that soon after Dr. Aafia and her children were arrested in 2003, she was released back into public, and for the missing 5 years of her journey she worked underground as a terrorist sympathizer, until she was finally detained in Ghazni with a bag of incriminating documents.

She wasn't charged with terrorism and so Judge Berman significantly limited the evidence and testimony on this subject.

Perhaps you would like to think about it as well?

Certain people are of the opinion that if Dr. Aafia had been released from a secret prison just before she arrived in Ghazni, then the bag of incriminating documents must have been planted on her; which she also claimed in her testimony. However, this testimony was never allowed to be developed or explored and thus remained largely ignored.

For many, the events taking place in Ghazni give rise to numerous questions. Why did the Afghanistan government allow Dr. Aafia to be extradited to America? Why didn't Hamid Karzai (the Afghanistan President at that time) inform Pakistan about what Dr. Aafia (a Pakistani citizen) was allegedly involved in?

As shared in this book, after being shot, Dr. Aafia stayed in Bagram hospital for two weeks. Why wasn't Pakistan's government contacted during that time? Many believe Afghanistan illegally detained Dr. Aafia (especially by not informing Pakistan). Furthermore, she was illegally extradited and thus Afghanistan was in violation of the Vienna Convention.

Such an occurrence leads to two major opinions. Either Afghanistan did violate the Vienna Convention or Pakistan was indeed notified about

Dr. Aafia and Pakistan allowed her to be taken to America as a person of interest in a terrorism-related case; some believe due to political pressure from the US.

Since forensic evidence showed Dr. Aafia didn't shoot at US soldiers, was the entire thing a ploy to have her extradited when the US soldiers weren't allowed to take her away when they first came to the Afghan Police station? Perhaps, Hamid Karzai would like to share the details?

Furthermore coming back to the trial, it has also been said Judge Berman's statements apparently came from unsworn comments from the prosecutors. At the same time, Judge Berman (allegedly) ignored clear evidence in the trial about how Dr. Aafia had been in a secret prison during the missing 5 years and couldn't have been engaged in terrorism-related work.

The Judge also gave Dr. Aafia an 86-year sentence which is far beyond a normal sentence for someone found guilty of attempted murder, where the crime arose spontaneously, a gun was fired, and nobody was hurt (except, as in this case, the person shooting the gun). Given the forensic evidence Dr. Aafia couldn't have fired at US soldiers.

Also, for some, Judge Berman allegedly continued to have a bias against Dr. Aafia. He was forthcoming about how her 2255 application would have been rejected even if she didn't request for it to be withdrawn. Judge Berman seemed to have presented a negative image of Dr. Aafia to the general public which led her to be branded as a terrorist in the public eye due to the Judge insinuating she was in Afghanistan only for terrorist activities.

Many believe a different Judge should handle Dr. Aafia's case because she has been vocal about how she didn't expect any justice from Judge Berman. For people who think this, they want a non-biased Judge to go over the trial and see if a different ruling can be presented.

Furthermore, the issue about Dr. Aafia's extrajudicial confessions to FBI agents regarding her alleged links with Al-Qaeda and other terrorist organizations as well as actions, while she was hospitalized at Bagram Airbase hospital, Afghanistan, remains. People think these confessions don't hold validity because these extrajudicial confessions weren't ever cross-examined in court by Aafia attorneys. It is as if a narrative has been fabricated to paint Dr. Aafia Siddiqui as FBI's Most Wanted Woman on a bias against Muslims.

But there is also the other side!

In contrast to all of this, certain people think Dr. Aafia is indeed guilty. For them, there are discrepancies in her story. Again, there is a lot of classified information involved, and people don't feel Dr. Aafia was completely truthful during her testimonies. For them, even if Dr. Aafia wasn't wholly involved with terrorist groups, she did have a role to play, even if it was just a minor one.

So, can her case move forward or will she complete her sentence of more than 80 years? The correct answer to such a question is a tough one.

There is a notion about there being a lack of curiosity and investigation by the Pakistan government about this case. It is as if the Pakistani government doesn't want to pursue Dr. Aafia's case wholeheartedly because they are either worried about action from the US government, are hiding something or they just don't care enough about freeing her.

Former Prime Minister Nawaz Sharif and the PPP government have been accused of not doing their best to free Dr. Aafia when they came into power in 2013. The current Prime Minister of Pakistan, Imran Khan, seems to be on the same route (I'll get to his July 2019 visit to the US in a bit.)

There is the question surrounding Dr. Aafia's third child named Soloman as well. He is, as of writing this book, still missing. Many people wonder why the government hasn't done anything of significance to find him.

It is also of interest to note Dr. Aafia's application for Commutation, which was pending before the President of the United States of America, has been denied. Dr. Aafia had not signed it which makes it a procedural matter.

There are some who believe she didn't sign it (and also, similarly, withdrew her 2255 petition) due to mental health issues. I have talked about Dr. Aafia and the confusion surrounding her PTSD in this book. For many, she isn't being given the proper treatment for her mental state. Her condition raises questions about the US Government's responsibility toward traumatized captives.

Why isn't she being properly treated for her PTSD even though she is being kept at the Federal Medical Center, Carswell? Why can't the treatment of a Pakistani citizen be done under supervision in Pakistan?

Her mental state is being analyzed as a reason for why she wishes to be repatriated, but she is also refusing to sign papers (that can help bring her home) due to PTSD-related fears. For those wondering how her case can continue, Pakistan can pursue another application before the U.S. President. In 2013, Pakistan failed to pursue Dr. Aafia's clemency application before President Obama when he pardoned many prisoners.

Yvonne Ridley continues to fight for Dr. Aafia's freedom. She shared her experience about being very close to having Dr. Aafia exchanged for an American soldier in Taliban custody, Robert "Bowe" Bergdahl. However, her efforts led her to a dead end due to the Pakistani establishment. Her story (published in May 2018) supports the notion many have about Pakistan's government not being interested in having Dr. Siddiqui released.

It is also interesting to add here that in July 2018 the Southern District of New York's Judge granted a new trial to the Uzair Paracha case while deciding the 2255 motion application. Remember, Dr. Aafia was an unindicted co-conspirator in that case.

The judge's decision was based on new evidence obtained from the declassified statements of Khalid Sheikh Muhammed, Majid Khan, and Ammar Al Baluchi which came after one year of the Uzair Paracha trial.

Due to such a change in Uzair Paracha's case, as a result of declassification of the information by the US government, it can bring more weight to Dr. Aafia narrative of being detained in a secret prison.

Many are keeping an eye on the Uzair Paracha case, especially due to what the US Supreme Court has done. Serving as a barrier against efforts to prosecute five Guantanamo Bay detainees (including Khalid Sheikh Mohammed and Majid Khan) who were accused of aiding in the 9/11 terrorist attacks, a military commissions judge ruled that a key piece of evidence against the men may not be used by prosecutors. The said evidence were the statements the men made to F.B.I interrogators "shortly" after being transferred from C.I.A.'s "black site" prisons.

Defense lawyers are interested in investigating the torture experienced by their clients from the C.I.A. Furthermore, many believe the statements made should not hold enough weight to grant someone a death penalty because they weren't cross-examined (especially face-to-face).

Numerous people (including certain Dr. Aafia's supporters) appreciate the decision made by the Supreme Court against Congress because for them, the Supreme Court shared a verdict not burdened with bias. There are people who believe if such a position wasn't taken by the Supreme Court, similar statements (made during torture) would have been used to convict numerous people by the US Congress to serve as examples against terrorism.

This has given supporters of Dr. Aafia Siddiqui that she too will, one day, have a fair trial.

The Guantanamo issue is something supporters of Dr. Aafia are keeping an eye on. A major decision, in April 2019, from the U.S. Court of Appeals for the D.C. Circuit essentially disqualified one of the key

Guantanamo Judges, Air Force Colonel Vance Spath, in the " Al-Nashiri" case (Abd al-Rahim al-Nashiri is a Saudi Arabian citizen alleged to be the mastermind of the bombing of *USS Cole* and other maritime terrorist attacks).

This was done due to Spath's misconduct and bias being tracked back a number of years. Turns out, Spath was "actively pursuing" employment from the Justice Department as an immigration judge during that time and didn't disclose it to the parties.

Such a decision invalidates all or most of Judge Spath's decisions incases he handled, more or less, over the last 5 years.[267] The said decision continues the conversation about the lawfulness of the Military Commissions. For many, the Military Commissions enterprise is a waste of money, labor, and time. For many, it is time to finally realize the Guantanamo Military Commissions have failed. It stands against what justice means in the American legal system.

Dr. Aafia's supporters are following the situation and waiting to see how, when, and if this decision impacts the other Guantanamo cases (including Paracha's).

In a more recent development, on April 25, 2019, Pakistan's Foreign Office Spokesperson Dr. Mohammed Faisal had to clarify his statement about how Dr. Aafia Siddiqui didn't want to come back to Pakistan. He said the statement had been taken out of context and "steps" to bring Dr. Aafia back were in motion.

Dr. Aafia's return all comes down to Prime Minister Imran Khan and U.S. President Donald Trump meeting in the future as that could lead to talks about the exchange of Dr. Aafia Siddiqui for Shakeel Afridi (which is a continuing issue).

Dr. Faisal ensures Pakistan's stance remains the same as before with regards to Dr. Aafia and Shakeel Afridi.

According to Dr. Aafia's sister, she does want to return to Pakistan and anyone saying otherwise shouldn't be trusted. However, Pakistan's government is yet to do anything of significance regarding the case.

Some are looking to US Senator Lindsey Graham (Chair of the Senate Committee on the Judiciary) to aid with the proceedings to have Dr. Aafia released. According to reports, Senator Graham was instrumental in making the July 2019 meeting between PM Imran Khan and President Trump occur. Senator Graham has also shown interest in handling the Afghan Peace Process and persuaded Pakistan to be a part of it. The US wants to continue (as well as expand) trade with Pakistan, too. Senator Graham's help with Dr. Aafia's release (whether it's through an exchange with Shakeel Afridi or via another route) can likely result in numerous positives.

But there's also a downside certain people are seeing related to Shakeel Afridi's case reaching Peshawar High Court. There is a likelihood of Afridi being released. If that happens, how will Aafia's 'swap' situation be handled?

During PM Imran Khan's visit to the U.S. in July 2019, he talked to President Trump about repairing the relationship between the two countries. Handling of peace in Afghanistan and Kashmir were prioritized issues. However, during a sit down with Fox News, PM Imran was asked about Afridi's fate which led to the PM bringing up Dr. Aafia on international TV. The PM's response does indicate freeing Dr. Siddiqui remains on the 'to-do' list, but the narrative surrounding her needs to be changed. Her situation needs to differ from just being a political prisoner waiting to be swapped.

What the U.S. needs to realize is holding Dr. Siddiqui as a political bargaining chip has continued to fuel a narrative by terrorist organizations (such as ISIS and Daesh) in which she has become an icon. Terrorist leaders use the plight of their "Muslim sister" to recruit more people in their fight for her freedom.

Dr. Aafia's repatriation under condition for peaceful means, as a peace agent, can help Pakistan to counter terrorist ideologies and can help end Dr. Aafia being used by terrorist organizations for their own gain. This suggestion has been given while considering Dr. Aafia's educational background, experience developing Adult educational programs, and her life long ambitions to teach children. If America agrees, then both countries can deal with the legal technicalities that would arise in repatriating Aafia to Pakistan.

Being a peace issue involving America, Pakistan, and Afghanistan, U.S. leadership needs to come together. Many want Senator Graham to be reached out to and to be explained the regional, social, and political benefits of Dr. Aafia's repatriation.

Dr. Aafia repatriation will be looked upon as a gesture of good faith from the U.S. for not only improving ties with Pakistan, but for also putting an end to the narrative terrorists have created in Dr. Aafia's name. Extreme efforts are required to lobby (both in the U.S. and Pakistan) with regards to the wide spreading peaceful impact of Dr. Aafia's repatriation. Obtaining such a goal is possible through mutual understanding and respect.

Can the healing of the Pakistani nation ever be complete without the repatriation of Dr. Aafia?

I can't provide you with a definitive answer.

However, what's ensured is Dr. Aafia's case will continue to be talked about in certain political and legal circles.

Dr. Aafia's family and several activist groups are still fighting for her freedom. Time will tell if their efforts bear any positive results.

Appendix

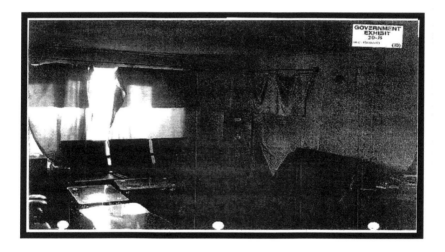

268

1. Second floor room at Afghan Police station Ghazni: Chairs against window walls where officers were seated at the time of the shooting event.

269

2. Second floor room at Afghan Police station Ghazni: location where Chief Warrant officer, Interior Ministry Officials, Captain Snyder, MacDonald & Williams were seated before shooting incident

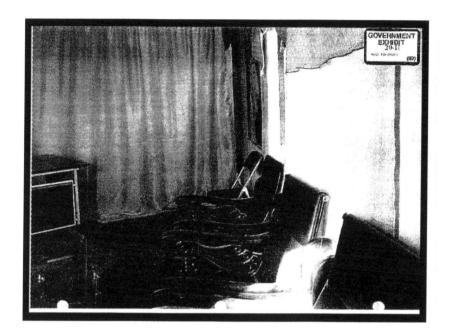

270

3. Second floor room at Afghan Police station Ghazni: Yellow
curtain dividing rooms with desk & seating where officers
were seated

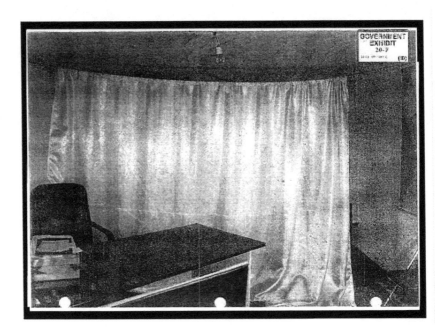

271

4. Second floor room at Afghan Police station Ghazni: Desk
   in front of yellow curtain dividing room

5. Second floor room at Afghan Police station Ghazni: Angled desk and chair to the left of main entry and located in front of yellow curtain separating

272

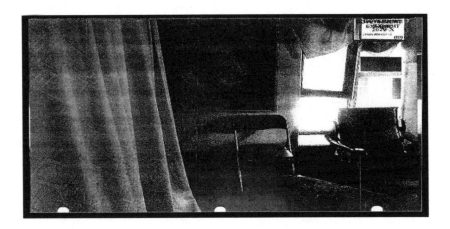

273

6. Second floor room at Afghan Police station Ghazni: Back Window wall with photo of President Karzai and chairs where the Chief Warrant Officer and Interior Ministry Officials were seated next to the yellow curtain before the shooting.

Acknowledgments

Special thanks goes to Syed Muhammad Younas, Farid Ul Haq, Saima Seyar, Meriam Sabih, Advocate Shah Khawar, Saad Mir Baggoo, Malik Shahbaz, Hassan Bhalli, Barrister Masood Muhammad, Shahid Comrade, Raja Yaqoob, Mohammed Chohan, Dr. Ashraf Abbasi, Qaiser Khan for your general assistance and encouragement. And finally thank you to the United States District Court for the Southern District of New York, Fowzia Siddiqui, and Attorney Kathy Manley for providing me the documents of the *United States of America v Aafia Siddiqui* case.

Notes

1 When I was a baby: *United States of America v Aafia Siddiqui.* Dated January 28, 2010. Pp 1695- 1697

2 Chemistry was actually: *United States of America v Aafia Siddiqui.* Dated January 28, 2010. Pp 1698- 1704

3 Before we returned: *United States of America v Aafia Siddiqui.* Dated January 28, 2010. Pp 1707- 1708

4 Period between 2003 and 2008: *United States of America v Aafia Siddiqui.* Dated November 19, 2008. Pp 4-5

5 We are not going to argue: *United States of America v Aafia Siddiqui.* Dated January 11, 2010. Pp 20

6 We are certainly not going to have: *United States of America v Aafia Siddiqui.* Dated November 19, 2008. Pp 8-11

7 Now the Allegations in: *United States of America v Aafia Siddiqui.* Dated November 19, 2008. Pp 11

8 There is no hard evidence: *United States of America v Aafia Siddiqui.* Dated November 19, 2008. Pp 12

9 He is heavily medicated: *United States of America v Aafia Siddiqui.* Dated November 19, 2008. Pp 17-20

10 There is a lawsuit in Islamabad: *United States of America v Aafia Siddiqui.* Dated November 19, 2008. Pp 20-23

11 The Guardian 2001, "Text of George Bush's Speech," viewed 25th Dec 2018, https://www.theguardian.com/world/2001/sep/21/september11.usa13

12 CBS NEWS 2001, Taliban Won't turn over Bin Laden, viewed 26th Dec 2018, https://www.cbsnews.com/news/taliban-wont-turn-over-bin-laden/

13 US Department of State, Cable, "Deputy Secretary Armitage's Meeting with Pakistan Intel Chief Mahmud: You're Either With Us or You're Not," September 13, 2001, Secret, 9 pp. [Excised]. https://nsarchive2.gwu.edu/NSAEBB/NSAEBB358a/doc03-1.pdf

14 U.S. Department of State Cable, "Deputy Secretary Armitage's meeting with General Mahmud: Actions and Support Expected of Pakistan in Fight Against Terrorism," September 14, 2001, Secret, 5 pp [Excised]. https://nsarchive2.gwu.edu/NSAEBB/NSAEBB358a/doc05.pdf

15 BBC 2001, Text: Musharaf rallies Pakistan, viewed 26th December 2018, http://news.bbc.co.uk/2/hi/world/monitoring/media_reports/1553542.stm

16 The Guardian 2006, *"Bush threatened to bomb Pakistan*, says Musharraf, viewed 26th December 2018, https://www.theguardian.com/world/2006/sep/22/pakistan.usa

17 BBC 2001, The US refuses to negotiate with the Taliban, viewed 26th Dec 2018, http://www.bbc.co.uk/history/events/the_us_refuses_to_negotiate_with_the_taliban

18 CNN 2001, *"Bush announces opening of attacks,"* viewed 26th December 2018, http://edition.cnn.com/2001/US/10/07/ret.attack.bush/

19 CNN 2001, *Bush announces 'most wanted' terrorist list*, viewed 25 Dec 2018, http://edition.cnn.com/2001/ALLPOLITICS/10/10/inv.most.wanted/index.html

20 The New York Times, *A NATION CHALLENGED : THE INVES-TIGATION; Ashcroft Is Centralizing Control Over the Prosecution and Prevention of Terrorism*, viewed 25 Dec 2018. https://www.nytimes.com/2001/10/10/us/nation-challenged-investigation-ashcroft-centralizing-control-over-prosecution.html

21 Musharraf, P. In the Line of Fire: a Memoir, New York, NY: Free Press: Simon and Schuster Digitals Sales Inc. pp 704-705

22 CNN 2003, Top Al Qaeda operative caught in Pakistan, viewed 29th December 2018, http://edition.cnn.com/2003/WORLD/asiapcf/south/03/01/pakistan.arrests/

23 Central Intelligence Agency's Detention and Interrogation Program with Chairman Feinstein 2014, Report of the Senate Select Committee on Intelligence Committee Study. Senate report 113-288. Viewed 29th December 2018. https://books.google.com.pk/books?id=YwJze-br8bPkC&pg=PA181&lpg=PA181&dq=aafia+named+placed+in+F-BI+list&source=bl&ots=XfYqVvPbEQ&sig=rbjHCsHMe15P9gjN-vW8rzxt4ffQ&hl=en&sa=X&ved=2ahUKEwjR0Nm1hsPfAhXyqHEK-Hc0NDms4HhDoATADegQICBAB#v=onepage&q=aafia%20named%20placed%20in%20FBI%20list&f=false

24 Bartosiewicz, P. (2009) The Intelligence Factory: How America makes its enemies disappear. HARPERS MAGAZINE. Viewed 30th December 2018. https://harpers.org/archive/2009/11/the-intelligence-factory/5/

25 Scroggins, D. (2012), *"WANTED WOMAN Faith, lies, and the War on Terror: The Lives of Ayaan Hirsi Ali and Aafia Siddiqui"*. An Imprint of HarperCollins Publishers. Pp Part II, Chapter 16, page 245

26 Human Rights Watch 2008, *"Afghanistan: Free Aafia Siddiqui's 11-year-old son "*, viewed 29th December 2018, https://www.hrw.org/news/2008/08/27/afghanistan-free-aafia-siddiquis-11-year-old-son

27 Internet Archive Wayback Machine, *"Seeking Information: War on terror,"* viewed 29th December 2018, https://web.archive.org/web/20030621164646/http://www.fbi.gov:80/terrorinfo/siddiqui.htm

28 Scroggins, D. (2012), *"WANTED WOMAN Faith, lies, and the War on Terror: The Lives of Ayaan Hirsi Ali and Aafia Siddiqui."* An Imprint of HarperCollins Publishers. Pp Part II, Chapter 6, page 185-186

29 Whether FBI questioned her: United States of America v Aafia Siddiqui, 28 November 2010, pp 1725- 1726

30 Complaint: United States of America v Uzair Paracha. 8th August 2003. https://www.investigativeproject.org/documents/case_docs/242.pdf

31 Scroggins, D. (2012), *"WANTED WOMAN Faith, lies, and the War on Terror: The Lives of Ayaan Hirsi Ali and Aafia Siddiqui."* An Imprint of HarperCollins Publishers. Pp Part II, Chapter 16, page 245

32 Dawn (2004), Letters: Dr Aafia Siddiqui disappearance. Viewed 01st January 2019. https://www.dawn.com/news/1065788

33 Scroggins, D. (2012), *"WANTED WOMAN Faith, lies, and the War on Terror: The Lives of Ayaan Hirsi Ali and Aafia Siddiqui."* An Imprint of HarperCollins Publishers. Pp Part II chapter 16, page 248

34 Ashfaque, A.U. (2003, March 31). FBI wanted woman held in Karachi. *The News International.*

35 Kuwait News Agency KUNA 2003, FBI Wanted Pakistani women detained. Viewed 29th December 2018. https://www.kuna.net.kw/ArticlePrintPage.aspx?id=1332877&language=en

36 Hassan, S.S. BBC (2008). "Mystery of Siddiqui Disappearance." Viewed 30th December 2018. http://news.bbc.co.uk/2/hi/south_asia/7544008.stm

37 Khattak, N.(2010, February,04). *Off The Record Imran Khan on Aafia Siddiqi: Part 2 of 5*[video file]. Retrieved from https://www.youtube.com/watch?v=CNKE2aqvdHE

38 NBC News. (2003,April).*Free Aafia* [Video file]. Retrieved from https://youtu.be/6xwCHha5ITM

39 Scroggins, D. (2012), *"WANTED WOMAN Faith, lies, and the War on Terror: The Lives of Ayaan Hirsi Ali and Aafia Siddiqui."* An Imprint of HarperCollins Publishers. Pp Part II chapter 16, page 250-251

40 Buncombe, A. (2018). Alleged 9/11 plotter held at Guantanamo illegally should be released immediately, says UN. Independent. Viewed 31st December 2018. https://www.independent.co.uk/news/world/americas/ammar-al-baluchi-9-11-plotter-un-release-guantanamo-gitmo-illegal-detention-a8233451.html

41 Schmitt, E (2008). " Pakistani suspected of Qaeda ties is held." The New York Times. Viewed on 31st December 2018. https://www.nytimes.com/2008/08/05/world/asia/05detain.html

42 The Washington Times 2003, Suspect in terror plot still at large. Viewed 30th December 2018. https://www.washingtontimes.com/news/2003/jun/16/20030616-104107-6807r/

43 Dawn 2004. Dr. Aafia was handed over to the US last year: Govt. viewed 30th December 2018. https://www.dawn.com/news/360381

44 The White house 2003. President Bush welcomes President Musharraf to Camp David. Viewed 30th December 2018. https://georgewbush-whitehouse.archives.gov/news/releases/2003/06/20030624-3.html

45 CNN (2004). Transcript: Ashcroft, Mueller news conference. Viewed 31st December 2018. http://edition.cnn.com/2004/US/05/26/terror.threat.transcript/

46 United States Attorney Southern District of New York (2006). PAKISTAN MAN CONVICTED OF PROVIDING MATERIAL SUPPORT TO AL QAEDA SENTENCED TO 30 YEARS IN FEDERAL PRISON", Viewed 31st December 2018. https://www.justice.gov/archive/usao/nys/pressreleases/July06/parachasentencingpr.pdf

47 Scroggins, D. (2012), *"WANTED WOMAN Faith, lies, and the War on Terror: The Lives of Ayaan Hirsi Ali and Aafia Siddiqui".* An Imprint of HarperCollins Publishers. Pp Part II, Chapter 14, page 231

48 Dawn (2004), Letters: Dr. Aafia Siddiqui disappearance. Viewed 01st January 2019. https://www.dawn.com/news/1065788

49 Priest, D (2005) CIA holds terror suspects in secret prisons. Washington Post. Viewed on 1st January 2019. http://www.washingtonpost.com/wp-dyn/content/article/2005/11/01/AR2005110101644.html

50 BBC (2014). CIA Tactics: What is enhanced interrogation". Viewed on 1st January 2019. https://www.bbc.com/news/world-us-canada-11723189

51 Chappel, B (2017). Psychologists behind CIA "Enhanced Interrogation Program Settle Detainees" Lawsuit. National Public Radio. Viewed on 1st January 2019. https://www.npr.org/sections/thetwo-way/2017/08/17/544183178/psychologists-behind-cia-enhanced-interrogation-program-settle-detainees-lawsuit

52 CNN (2014). CIA Torture Report Fast Facts. Viewed on 1st January 2019. https://edition.cnn.com/2015/01/29/us/cia-torture-report-fast-facts/index.html

53 Mazzetti, M. (2014) Panel Fault CIA over Brutality and Deceit in Terrorism Interrogations. *The New York Times.* https://www.nytimes.com/2014/12/10/world/senate-intelligence-committee-cia-torture-report.html

54 Relax: *United States of America v Aafia Siddiqui,* January 28, 2010, pp 1760-1762

55 Open Society Foundations (2013). Investigations into CIA Renditions. Viewed on 1st January 2019. https://www.opensocietyfoundations.org/fact-sheets/investigations-cia-renditions

56 an Society Foundations. Open Society Justice Initiative. (2013). *Globalizing Torture: CIA Secret Detention And Extraordinary Rendition.* Pg 6. https://www.opensocietyfoundations.org/sites/default/files/globalizing-torture-20120205.pdf

57 Edwards, A. &Ferstman,C.(2010,March 26). *Human Security and Non-Citizens: Law Policy and International Affairs.* Pg 15.Cambridge University Press. https://books.google.com.pk/books?id=yvQfAwAAQBAJ&pg=PA532&lpg=PA532&dq=andrews+Air+Force+Base,+December+5,+2005:+%22Rice+Says+United+States+Does+Not+Torture+Terrorists.+Secretary+says+%27rendition%27+vital,+legal+tool+to+combat+terrorism,+save+lives&source=bl&ots=koAXqmT-Ib&sig=Nn_M9YQgRbHNvvYfzFnojPBj9e8&hl=en&sa=X&ved=2ahUKEwj0gJLaq83fAhWlunEKHXiqDIAQ6AEwBHoECAUQAQ#v=onepage&q=andrews%20Air%20Force%20Base%2C%20December%205%2C%202005%3A%20%22Rice%20Says%20United%20States%20Does%20Not%20Torture%20Terrorists.%20Secretary%20says%20'rendition'%20vital%2C%20legal%20tool%20to%20combat%20terrorism%2C%20save%20lives&f=false

58 BBC (2006). *"Bush admits to CIA secret prisons."* Viewed on 01 January 2019. http://news.bbc.co.uk/2/hi/americas/5321606.stm

59 American Rhetoric Online Speech Bank (2006) George W Bush speech on Military Commissions to try suspected terrorists. Viewed 1st January 2019. https://www.americanrhetoric.com/speeches/gwbushmilitarytribunalsforterrorists.htm

60 EXTRAORDINARY RENDITION IN U.S. COUNTERTERRORISM POLICY: THE IMPACT ON TRANSATLANTIC RELATIONS: *JOINT HEARING BEFORE THE SUBCOMMITTEE ON INTERNATIONAL ORGANISATIONS, HUMAN RIGHTS, AND OVERSIGHT AND THE SUBCOMMITTEE ON EUROPE OF THE COMMITTEE ON FOREIGN AFFAIRS HOUSE OF REPRESENTATIVES.* (Serial No. 110-28), 110th Cong. (2007).

61 International Justice Network (2011) Aafia Siddiqui: Just the facts A report of the International Justice Network. Viewed 31st December 2018. file:///C:/Users/ma/Downloads/AfiaReport-web-100411_2.pdf

62 Bartosiewicz, P. (2009) The Intelligence Factory: How America makes its enemies disappear. HARPERS MAGAZINE. Viewed 30th December 2018. https://harpers.org/archive/2009/11/the-intelligence-factory/6/\

63 Taylor, R.N. (2014) The Strange case of MoazzamBegg. The Guardian. Viewed on 3rd January 2019. https://www.theguardian.com/world/defence-and-security-blog/2014/oct/07/moazzam-begg-mi5-syria

64 Mayer, J. (2006). The Accused. The Washington Post. Viewed on 3rd January 2019. http://www.washingtonpost.com/wp-dyn/content/article/2006/09/07/AR2006090701109.html

65 Begg, M. &Brittain, V. (2007). Enemy Combatant: My Imprisonment at Guantanamo, Bagram, and Kandahar. New Press. Pp 251-253

66 Q Dr. Siddiqui: *United States of America v Aafia Siddiqui,* January 28, 2010, pp 1665

67 What is this: *United States of America v Aafia Siddiqui*, January 28, 2010, pp 1710-1711

68 Now, this document: *United States of America v Aafia Siddiqui,* January 28, 1730

69 BBC (2001). The Journalist and the Taleban. Viewed 3rd January 2019. http://www.bbc.co.uk/worldservice/people/highlights/011030_ridley.shtml

70 thugs: Yvonne Ridley. Viewed 3rd January 2019. https://www.hhugs.org.uk/2010/01/yvonne-ridley/

71 Downrodeo85. (2010, November 28).*In Search of Prisoner 650*[Video file]. Retrieved from https://youtu.be/TxHJ0IyKZ2Q

72 Mariner, J. (2008). The strange and Terrible case of Aafia Siddiqui. FindLaw for Legal Professionals. Viewed on 3rd January 2019. https://supreme.findlaw.com/legal-commentary/the-strange-and-terrible-case-of-aafia-siddiqui.html

73 Scroggins, D. (2012), *"WANTED WOMAN Faith, lies, and the War on Terror: The Lives of Ayaan Hirsi Ali and Aafia Siddiqui."* An Imprint of Harper Collins Publishers. Pp Part III, chapter 21, page 393

74 Yvonne Ridley Analysis & Opinion. Hoover, the FBI, and Aafia Siddiqui. Viewed on 4th January 2019. https://yvonneridley.org/analysis-and-opinion/hoover-the-fbi-and-aafia-siddiqui/

75 Scroggins, D. (2012), *"WANTED WOMAN Faith, lies, and the War on Terror: The Lives of Ayaan Hirsi Ali and Aafia Siddiqui."* An Imprint of HarperCollins Publishers. Pp Part III, chapter 21, page 395

76 Shahid, J. (2008) Pakistani woman languishing in Bagram. Dawn newspaper. Viewed on 4th January 2019. https://www.dawn.com/news/310586

77 Shahid, J (2008). No Woman Prisoner in Bagram, Says US. Dawn Newspaper. Viewed on 4th January 2019. https://www.dawn.com/news/311388

78 Downrodeo85. (2010, November 28).*In Search of Prisoner 650*[Video file]. Retrieved from https://youtu.be/TxHJ0IyKZ2Q

79 Jaffry, N. (2008). The Tortured life of Bagram Grey lady. The Telegraph. Viewed on 4th January 2019. https://www.telegraphindia.com/world/the-tortured-life-of-bagram-s-grey-lady/cid/558277

80 Downrodeo85. (2010, November 28).*In Search of Prisoner 650*[Video file]. Retrieved from https://youtu.be/TxHJ0IyKZ2Q

81 Scroggins, D. (2012), *"WANTED WOMAN Faith, lies, and the War on Terror: The Lives of Ayaan Hirsi Ali and Aafia Siddiqui."* An Imprint of HarperCollins Publishers. Pp Part III, chapter 27, page 420

82 The Asian Human Rights Commission (2008, August 08) *Dr. Afia's health is in serious condition and two of her children remain missing.* Urgent Appeal Case : AHRC-UAU-049-2008. Viewed on 1st May 2019. http://www.humanrights.asia/news/urgent-appeals/AHRC-UAU-049-2008/

83 Goldberg,S. &Shah.S (2008). Mystery of "ghost Bagram" – victim of Torture or captured in a shootout. Viewed on 4th January 2019. https://www.theguardian.com/world/2008/aug/06/pakistan.afghanistan

84 Downrodeo85. (2010, November 28). *In Search of Prisoner 650*[Video file]. Retrieved from https://youtu.be/TxHJ0IyKZ2Q

85 Amnesty International UK (2017) Binyam Mohamed. Viewed on 4th January 2019. https://www.amnesty.org.uk/binyam-mohamed

86 Begg, M.(2009, March 26). *Moazzam Begg in Conversation with Binyam Mohamed: Cageprisoners.* http://humanrights.ucdavis.edu/projects/the-guantanamo-testimonials-project/testimonies/prisoner-testimonies/moazzam-begg-in-conversation-with-binyam-mohamed

87 PressTVUKvideos. (2009, April 3). *Binyam Mohamed says prisoner 650 is Dr Aafia Siddiqui*[Video file]. Retrieved from https://youtu.be/OGHWcPRBQr8

88 Dawn (2010), *Aafia Siddiqui daughter*, retrieved 30 December 2018. https://www.dawn.com/news/878987

89 Many times I have said: *United States of America v Aafia Siddiqui*, January 28 2010, pp 1610

90 On or about *United States of America v Aafia Siddiqui*. Document 1, pp 1 -4

91 . He was working in the counterterrorism department: *United States of America v Aafia Siddiqui*, January 29, 2010, pp 1795 - 1803

92 I was a liaison officer: *United States of America v Aafia Siddiqui*, January 19, 2010, pp 237 – 255

93 The First thing we did: *United States of America v Aafia Siddiqui*, January 19, 2010, pp 128

94 I have never seen: *United States of America v Aafia Siddiqui*, January 25, 2010, pp 1009 – 1010

95 Particularly because of their: *United States of America v Aafia Siddiqui*, January 19, 2010, pp 129

96 I was put in contact: *United States of America v Aafia Siddiqui*, January 25, 2010, pp 1011

97 This morning I was contact: *United States of America v Aafia Siddiqui*, January 25, 2010, pp 1140 – 1142

98 Once we arrived in Ghazni: *United States of America v Aafia Siddiqui*, January 25, 2010, pp 1143

99 The meeting took place: *United States of America v Aafia Siddiqui*, January 19, 2010, pp 279

100 Well, this morning my battalion: *United States of America v Aafia Siddiqui*, January 19 2010, pp 130

101 The reason why we were trying: *United States of America v Aafia Siddiqui*, January 19, 2010, pp 280-283

102 We went back to the base: *United States of America v Aafia Siddiqui*, January 25, 2010, pp 1015

103 I recontacted the warrant officer: *United States of America v Aafia Siddiqui*, January 25, 2010, pp 1146

104 We traveled to the Afghan National: *United States of America v Aafia Siddiqui*, January 19 2010, pp 284

105 I had my M4: *United States of America v Aafia Siddiqui*, January 19, 2010, pp 139

106 I was wearing military fatigues: *United States of America v Aafia Siddiqui*, January 25, 2010, pp 1149

107 I was wearing known as *United States of America v Aafia Siddiqui*, January 25, 2010, pp 1066-1067

108 I had my helmet: *United States of America v Aafia Siddiqui*, January 25, 2010, pp 950

109 I was always carrying AK-47: *United States of America v Aafia Siddiqui*, January 20, 2010, pp 409

110 I had on my body armor: *United States of America v Aafia Siddiqui*, January 26, 2010, pp 1323

111 We went straight there: *United States of America v Aafia Siddiqui*, January 26, 2010, pp 1376

112 Headquarter surrounded by: *United States of America v Aafia Siddiqui*, January 19, 2010, pp 285

113 I posted security to the door: *United States of America v Aafia Siddiqui*, January 26, 2010, pp 1384

114 They told us that no senior representative: *United States of America v Aafia Siddiqui*, January 19, 2010, pp 142

115 I realized that the overall provincial commander: *United States of America v Aafia Siddiqui*, January 25, 2010, pp 1064 – 1066

116 The Representative from NDS returned: *United States of America v Aafia Siddiqui*, January 19, 2010, pp 145 – 147

117 After he made a couple of phone calls: *United States of America v Aafia Siddiqui*, January 25, 2010, pp 1067-1069

118 As I was standing in the doorway: *States of America v Aafia Siddiqui*, January 25, 2010, pp 960 – 962

119 Was the room carpeted: *States of America v Aafia Siddiqui*, January 19, 2010, pp 291

120 There were several chairs: *United States of America v Aafia Siddiqui*, January 19, 2010, pp 149

121 Its President Hamid Karzai: *United States of America v Aafia Siddiqui*, January 19, 2010, pp 159

122 It separated the room: *United States of America v Aafia Siddiqui*, January 25, 2010, pp 1174

123 I looked for a seat: *United States of America v Aafia Siddiqui*, January 25, 2010, pp 1069 – 1084

124 I pushed her against the wall: *United States of America v Aafia Siddiqui*, January 20, pp 427

125 Once the interpreter removed the curtain: *United States of America v Aafia Siddiqui*, January 25, 2010, pp 1181 - 1183

126 She continued to fight: *United States of America v Aafia Siddiqui*, January 19, 2010, pp 177

127 I called for a medic to come: *United States of America v Aafia Siddiqui*, January 25, 2010, pp 1184-1185

128 I went ahead lifted her top : *United States of America v Aafia Siddiqui*, January 25, 2010, pp 972 – 974

129 Looked out of the window: *United States of America v Aafia Siddiqui*, January 25, 2010, pp 1085

130 We decided to start moving: *United States of America v Aafia Siddiqui*, January 26, 2010, pp 1186

131 Kevin Snyder and other gentlemen: *United States of America v Aafia Siddiqui*, January 25, 2010, pp 977 -978

132 As soon as we came out: *United States of America v Aafia Siddiqui*, January 26, 2010, pp 1189

133 When we got downstairs: *United States of America v Aafia Siddiqui*, January 25, 2010, pp 977

134 Once we got outside: *United States of America v Aafia Siddiqui*, January 19, 2010, pp 185-186

135 There was some questions: *United States of America v Aafia Siddiqui,* January 19, 2010, pp 186

136 When I arrived at Aid station: *United States of America v Aafia Siddiqui*, January 25, 2010, pp 979 – 980

137 Just stood outside waiting: *United States of America v Aafia Siddiqui*, January 26, 2010, pp 1194 - 1201

138 Once she was brought to the hospital: *United States of America v Aafia Siddiqui*, January 29, 2010, pp 1852

139 She has these soft's: *United States of America v Aafia Siddiqui,* January 28, 2010, pp 1642

140 Once a subject is brought into FBI : *United States of America v Aafia Siddiqui*, January 29 2010, pp 1870-1871.

141 Aafia Siddiqui was arrested: *United States of America v Aafia Siddiqui*, January 28, 2010, pp 1619 – 1623

142 She indicated that she enjoyed: *United States of America v Aafia Siddiqui*, January 28, 2010, pp 1623 - 1625

143 Discussions with the Defendant: *United States of America v Aafia Siddiqui February 01*, 2010, pp 1914

144 She said she had documents: *United States of America v Aafia Siddiqui February 01*, 2010, pp 1912 - 1913

145 She asked me what the penalty: *United States of America v Aafia Siddiqui February 01*, 2010, pp 1915 - 1916

146 I spoke to her on 21st of July: *United States of America v Aafia Siddiqui January 29*, 2010, pp 1854 – 1856

147 I am not afraid of speaking truth: *United States of America v Aafia Siddiqui January 28*, 2010, pp 1708 – 1709

148 What is my first memory: *United States of America v Aafia Siddiqui January 28*, 2010, pp 1710 – 1711

149 The night before there was Americans: *United States of America v Aafia Siddiqui January 28*, 2010, pp 1738

150 Over there again: *United States of America v Aafia Siddiqui January 28*, 2010, pp 1715

151 There was a lot of people: *United States of America v Aafia Siddiqui January 28* 2010, pp 1711 – 1714

152 She moved towards the Curtain: *United States of America v Aafia Siddiqui January 28*, 2010, pp 1716 – 1717

153 So at times I remember hearing: *United States of America v Aafia Siddiqui January 28*, 2010, pp 1718 – 1719

154 Siddiqui did you ever: *United States of America v Aafia Siddiqui January 28*, 2010, pp 1719,1720, 1742

155 I was there with a boy: *United States of America v Aafia Siddiqui January 28*, 2010, pp 1726 – 1732

156 At MIT she probably could have: *United States of America v Aafia Siddiqui January 28*, 2010, pp 1732 - 1733

157 God cured me: *United States of America v Aafia Siddiqui January 28*, 2010, pp 1743

158 Do you recall a time: *United States of America v Aafia Siddiqui January 28*, 2010, pp 1656 - 1659

159 At any time did any person: *United States of America v Aafia Siddiqui January 28*, 2010, pp 1659 – 1663

160 She did give the phone number: *United States of America v Aafia Siddiqui January 28*, 2010, pp 1663 – 1668

161 You were able to talk: *United States of America v Aafia Siddiqui January 28*, 2010, pp 1668 – 1671

162 I told him that: *United States of America v Aafia Siddiqui January 29*, 2010, pp 1744

163 No, it is not true: *United States of America v Aafia Siddiqui January 29*, 2010, pp 1747 - 1755

164 . This woman that has grabbed: *United States of America v Aafia Siddiqui.* January 25, 2010, pp 1077- 1078

165 What I saw was a female: *United States of America v Aafia Siddiqui.* January 19, 2010, pp 166- 174

166 Two hands and began to fire: *United States of America v Aafia Siddiqui.* January 26, 2010, pp 166- 174

167 I saw a female holding: *United States of America v Aafia Siddiqui.* January 20, 2010, pp 427-428

168 I saw the woman: *United States of America v Aafia Siddiqui.* January 25, 2010, pp 968

169 Get the fuck out of here : *United States of America v Aafia Siddiqui.* January 26, 2010, pp 1270- 1276

170 Ever picked up a rifle: *United States of America v Aafia Siddiqui.* January 28, 2010, pp 1720-1776

171 We heard gunfire: *United States of America v Aafia Siddiqui.* January 21, 2010, pp 1808- 1812

172 Assigned to Investigate: *United States of America v Aafia Siddiqui.* January 21, 2010, pp 602 -612

173 . Once we got everyone: *United States of America v Aafia Siddiqui.* January 21, 2010, pp 619

174 The wall the very brief: *United States of America v Aafia Siddiqui.* January 21, 2010, pp 630- 638

175 We tried to excavate: *United States of America v Aafia Siddiqui.* January 21, 2010, pp 644- 653

176 I collected an M4*: United States of America v Aafia Siddiqui.* January 21, 2010, pp 657

177 We wanted to do a: *United States of America v Aafia Siddiqui.* January 21, 2010, pp 680- 707

178 Did not find any evidence: *United States of America v Aafia Siddiqui.* January 21, 2010, pp 755

179 I was firearm and toolmark: *United States of America v Aafia Siddiqui.* January 22, 2010, pp 815- 828

180 I can identify M9: *United States of America v Aafia Siddiqui.* January 22, 2010, pp 828- 851

181 A bag of debris: *United States of America v Aafia Siddiqui*. January 22, 2010, pp 871-873

182 Photographs from the crime scene: *United States of America v Aafia Siddiqui*. January 22, 2010, pp 877-878

183 I worked at the FBI: *United States of America v Aafia Siddiqui*. January 20, 2010, pp 506-540

184 Mr. Tobin as an expert: *United States of America v Aafia Siddiqui*. January 27, 2010, pp 1430-1438

185 13 grain of powder: *United States of America v Aafia Siddiqui*. January 27, 2010, pp 1482- 1492

186 . You have no scientific doubts: *United States of America v Aafia Siddiqui*. January 27, 2010, pp 1476

187 I am Judge Ellis: *United States of America v Aafia Siddiqui*. Dated August 05 2008, pp 3-5

188 I understand them: *United States of America v Aafia Siddiqui*. Dated August 05 2008, pp 12 – 19

189 When she left Afghanistan: *United States of America v Aafia Siddiqui*. Dated August 05 2008, pp 21

190 I do like to introduce: *United States of America v Aafia Siddiqui*. Dated August 11, 2008, pp 2 - 5

191 She needs to be taken: *United States of America v Aafia Siddiqui*. Dated August 11, 2008, pp 10

192 A counselor from Washington: *United States of America v Aafia Siddiqui*. Dated August 11, 2008, pp 5 – 6

193 . Ms Sharp is an Expert: *United States of America v Aafia Siddiqui*. Dated August 11, 2008, pp 7 – 8

194 I am directing that: *United States of America v Aafia Siddiqui*. Dated August 11, 2008, pp 12

195 On or about *United States of America v Aafia Siddiqui*. Document 1, pp 1 -4

196 She was handcuffed: *United States of America v Aafia Siddiqui*. Document 10, pp 4-6

197 .. Dr Siddiqui is completely isolated: *United States of America v Aafia Siddiqui*. Document 10, pp 6

198 We are for arraignment today: *United States of America v Aafia Siddiqui*. September 04 2008, pp 2, 20

199 She is unbelievably damaged: *United States of America v Aafia Siddiqui*. September 04 2008, pp 17 – 19

200 There are gynecological: *United States of America v Aafia Siddiqui*. September 04 2008, pp 29

201 One thing I would ask for *United States of America v Aafia Siddiqui*. September 04 2008, pp 35 – 36

202 .. It is hereby ordered: *United States of America v Aafia Siddiqui*. Document 9, pp 1

203 Today a female doctor: *United States of America v Aafia Siddiqui*. Document 11, pp 1

204 BOP to perform: *United States of America v Aafia Siddiqui*. Document 11, pp 1

205 Shall include a forensic: *United States of America v Aafia Siddiqui*. Document 12, pp 1

206 McLean performed a psychological examination: *United States of America v Aafia Siddiqui*. Document 13, pp 1-2

207 I am writing this letter: *United States of America v Aafia Siddiqui*. Document 16, pp 1-3

208 The standard for determining: *United States of America v Aafia Siddiqui*. Document 17, pp 2-3

209 The Government believes that: *United States of America v Aafia Siddiqui*. Document 17, pp 1, pp 3, pp 6

210 The government has an opportunity: *United States of America v Aafia Siddiqui*. September 23, 2008, pp 2-3

211 . She's not competent: *United States of America v Aafia Siddiqui*. September 23, 2008, pp 5

212 I think it was September 10th: *United States of America v Aafia Siddiqui*. September 23, 2008, pp 16, pp 23

213 Upon the record of these proceedings: *United States of America v Aafia Siddiqui*. Document 21, pp 1 - 2

214 Pursuant to court order: *United States of America v Aafia Siddiqui*. Document 24, pp 1

215 During the court of this evaluation: *United States of America v Aafia Siddiqui*. Document 65, pp 1-8

216 The mental health professionals shall: *United States of America v Aafia Siddiqui*. Document 31, pp 2-3

217 The government retained two psychiatrists: *United States of America v Aafia Siddiqui*. Document 41, pp 1-2

218 I was asked by the United States: *United States of America v Aafia Siddiqui*. Document 58 pp 1-37

219 Evaluation procedures: *United States of America v Aafia Siddiqui*. Document 59 pp 2-35

220 In the absence of collateral: *United States of America v Aafia Siddiqui*. Document 60 pp 12

221 Dr. Siddiqui was interviewed: *United States of America v Aafia Siddiqui*. Document 61, pp 5

222 Throughout the records: *United States of America v Aafia Siddiqui*. Document 61, pp 5-6

223 . It is my opinion: *United States of America v Aafia Siddiqui*. Document 61, pp 13-15

224 Competency hearing was held on *United States of America v Aafia Siddiqui*. Document 74, pp 13 - 17

225 Elaine Sharp who is an attorney: *United States of America v Aafia Siddiqui*. August 5, 2008, pp 2-5

226 I would ask that: *United States of America v Aafia Siddiqui*. August 11, 2008, pp 2

227 Last but certainly not least: *United States of America v Aafia Siddiqui*. September 4, 2008, pp 5-13

228 She can't make a mental determination: *United States of America v Aafia Siddiqui*. September 23, 2008, pp 5-7

229 The government has an opportunity: *United States of America v Aafia Siddiqui*. September 23, 2008, pp 2-3

230 During the court of this evaluation: *United States of America v Aafia Siddiqui*. Document 65, pp 1-8

231 There are Pakistani legal groups: *United States of America v Aafia Siddiqui*. Document 60. Pp 10

232 Ms Siddiqui attorney: *United States of America v Aafia Siddiqui*. Document 59. Pp 33

233 Fink advised the court: *United States of America v Aafia Siddiqui*. February 23, 2009. Pp 2

234 Competency hearing was held on: *United States of America v Aafia Siddiqui*. Document 74, pp 13 - 17

235 Following this court determination: *United States of America v Aafia Siddiqui*. Document 76, pp 1-2

236 The government respectfully proposed: *United States of America v Aafia Siddiqui*. Document 82, pp 1-4

237 In response to government letter: *United States of America v Aafia Siddiqui*. Document 81 pp 1-2

238 So here are the issues: *United States of America v Aafia Siddiqui*. September 2, 2009, pp 5-30

239 There has been in my opinion: *United States of America v Aafia Siddiqui*. September 23, 2009, pp 4-20

240 I have relieved: *United States of America v Aafia Siddiqui*. Document 117, pp 1

241 We will take up: *United States of America v Aafia Siddiqui*. Document 117, pp 1

242 The first thing I want to mention: *United States of America v Aafia Siddiqui*. November 03, 2009, pp 2-8, 75-90

243 Following the hearing held: *United States of America v Aafia Siddiqui*. Document 122. Pp 1-9

244 It is torture for me: *United States of America v Aafia Siddiqui*. November 19, 2009, pp 33-36

245 . The government made a request: *United States of America v Aafia Siddiqui*. Dated January 11, 2009, pp 3-4, 69

246 I am only quiet because: *United States of America v Aafia Siddiqui*. January 13, 2010, pp 15-16

247 I need to have a conversation: *United States of America v Aafia Siddiqui*. January 19 2010, pp 60-65, 68-69

248 Siddiqui has the right: *United States of America v Aafia Siddiqui*. January 20 2010, pp 330-334, 346-349

249 Some time ago the US: *United States of America v Aafia Siddiqui*. January 25 2010, pp 1155- 1156, 1160

250 The deputy clerk asked: *United States of America v Aafia Siddiqui*. Dated February 3, 2010. Pp 2129- 2131

251 This was a very complicated: *United States of America v Aafia Siddiqui*. Dated September 23, 2010. Pp 16-19, pp 6, pp, pp 14

252 The upshot of my analysis: *United States of America v Aafia Siddiqui*. Dated September 23, 2010. Pp 91-93

253 I am recommending that she be: *United States of America v Aafia Siddiqui*. Dated September 23, 2010. Pp 106

254 I just want to: *United States of America v Aafia Siddiqui*. September 23, 2010. Pp 45-61

255 I have to clarify just one thing: *United States of America v Aafia Siddiqui*. September 23, 2010. Pp 87-91

256 I just want to say one thing: *United States of America v Aafia Siddiqui*. September 23, 2010. Pp 102-103

257 . You have the right to appeal: *United States of America v Aafia Siddiqui*. September 23, 2010. Pp 107-109

258 , This is a motion pursuant to: *Aafia Siddiqui v United States of America*. Document 8. Pp 1, 61-63

259 Mr. Boyle as counsel for Aafia: *Aafia Siddiqui v United States of America*. July 8, 2014 . Pp 2-3

260 Based upon the record: *Aafia Siddiqui v United States of America*. Document 7. Pp 1

261 Please be advised: Aafia *Siddiqui v United States of America*. Document 12-1. Pp 1

262 I participated in unmonitored: *Aafia Siddiqui v United States of America*. Document 14. Pp 2

263 To whom it may concern: *Aafia Siddiqui v United States of America*. Document 13-1. Pp 1

264 As to the recusal motion: *Aafia Siddiqui v United States of America*. Dated July 8, 2014. Pp 7-11

265 I hereby withdraw my 2255: *Aafia Siddiqui v United States of America*. Document 25. Pp 1

266 The letter from Aafia: Aafia Siddiqui v United States of America. Document 34. Pp 3

267 Grant, S (2019). " SUMMARY : D.C. CIRCUIT VACATES MILITARY JUDGE 'S RULING IN AL-NASHIRI". LAWFARE. Viewed on June 23 2019. https://www.lawfareblog.com/summary-dc-circuit-vacates-military-judges-rulings-al-nashiri

268 Government Exhibit 20B: *United States of America v Aafia Siddiqui*. Pp 36

269 Government Exhibit 20X: United States of America v Aafia Siddiqui. Pp 44

270 Government Exhibit 20H: *United States of America v Aafia Siddiqui*. Pp 39

271 Government Exhibit 20F: *United States of America v Aafia Siddiqui*. Pp 38

272 Government Exhibit 20HH. *United States of America v Aafia Siddiqui*. Pp 51

273 Government Exhibit 20Y: *United States of America v Aafia Siddiqui*. Pp 45